EXTREME SCIENCE

LARRY VERSTRAETE

Illustrations by
PAUL MCCUSKER
Design by
ANDREA CASAULT

SCHOLASTIC CANADA LTD.

Scholastic Canada Ltd.
175 Hillmount Rd., Markham, Ontario Canada L6C 1Z7

Scholastic Inc.
555 Broadway, New York NY 10012, USA

Scholastic Australia Pty Limited
PO Box 579, Gosford, NSW 2250, Australia

Scholastic New Zealand Ltd.
Private Bag 94407, Greenmount, Auckland, New Zealand

Scholastic Ltd.
Villiers House, Clarendon Avenue, Leamington Spa,
Warwickshire CV32 5PR, UK

CAUTION: Do not try to duplicate any of the experiments
or demonstrations described in this book at home.

Canadian Cataloguing in Publication Data
Verstraete, Larry
Extreme science
ISBN 0-590-24847-2

1. Discoveries in science — Juvenile literature. 2. Inventions — Juvenile literature.
3. Scientists – Biography – Juvenile literature. I. Title.
Q180.55.D57V47 2000   j500   C99-932686-4

5 4 3 2 1   Printed in Canada   0 1 2 3 4/0

For those brave and bold,
who extend the boundaries of our understanding

Acknowledgments

Isaac Newton, the famous English scientist, is often credited with saying: "If I have seen further, it is by standing on the shoulders of giants." Certainly this is true for scientists and inventors who constantly build on the work of others. It is also true for writers like myself who rely on eyewitness accounts and scientific reports to tell stories of scientists' adventures. I am indebted to these "giants" not only for their faithfulness to detail and accuracy, but also to their courage and ingenuity in the face of overwhelming odds.

I am also grateful to many others who helped me throughout the writing of this book.

To the Scholastic Canada team — Sandy Bogart Johnston, whose insights, sound advice and steady hand guided me on the long journey; designer Andrea Casault, who set the manuscript into its final form; and Rosemary Toth, who ensured that the information was precise and accurate — my sincerest thanks. To family, friends and colleagues whose interest in my writing is support itself, thank you for your questions and suggestions. And finally, but neither last nor least, thank you to my home team — Jo, Steven and Ashley — for their continued understanding and encouragement.

TAble of Contents

INtroduction

Don't be afraid of opposition. Remember, a kite rises
against — not with — the wind.

Hamilton Mabie

In 1942 a three-man suicide squad sat atop a pile of radioactive
uranium, ready to take drastic measures in case the experiment —
the world's first nuclear chain reaction — went horribly wrong. The
three physicists were ready to put their lives on the line to advance
the frontiers of science.

Almost four hundred years earlier, Italian astronomer Giordano
Bruno had faced another kind of ordeal. Bruno lived just before the
turn of the seventeenth century, a dangerous time for anyone with
new ideas. Those who held different views were often branded as
heretics, teachers of falsehood. The punishment for being a heretic
was severe: sometimes imprisonment, often death. So when Bruno
wrote a book that suggested life might exist on other planets besides
earth — a shocking concept to many — he was taking an enormous
risk. He was arrested, tried and found guilty of heresy. Giordano
Bruno was burned at the stake on February 17, 1600.

Science has its own special brand of heroes — people like the
three men on top of the nuclear reactor, armed with little more than
faith in their own logic — brave people like Bruno who challenge
established ways. To do the job that science demands, scientists and
inventors sometimes assume risks, take unusual steps, and attempt
the bold and impossible. They go to extremes for the sake of
discovery.

1

1

EXtreme EXperiments

Unravelling the truth . . .
providing proof

The **important thing** is not to stop questioning.

Albert Einstein

Most experiments are carefully planned events designed to provide answers to questions. Usually experiments involve exacting measurements — lots of them —and they're conducted in laboratories under safe, controlled conditions.

But not always. Some experiments are more extreme. Like Jake Socha's.

For his research project, Socha tossed snakes from a third-storey balcony. Flying snakes, that is. Poisonous ones.

Jake Socha, a graduate student at the University of Chicago, had an interest in the mildly poisonous paradise tree snake. In its native Asian habitat, the slender metre-long snake hunts for food and dodges enemies by flinging itself from one tree to the next. But did the paradise tree snake really fly? If it did, how? To find out, Socha designed an unusual experiment.

He constructed a launching station using a cardboard box with a sliding back wall. Then he perched the box on a third-floor balcony, put one of the snakes inside, and by sliding the rear wall, gently pushed the snake out.

Socha videotaped four snakes and seventy-four separate flights. He found that the tree snake doesn't really fly. It glides. As the snake leaps forward, it flattens itself to increase its surface area. Then it flexes and stretches its muscles, twisting itself in mid-air in order to propel and steer itself.

A strange experiment, but useful. To find answers, sometimes scientists — wisely or not — resort to unusual methods. Their experiments go one step farther than normal. They go to extremes.

Struck by Lightning

When storm clouds blew over Philadelphia in the summer of 1752, most people headed indoors.

Not Benjamin Franklin. He went outside to fly his kite.

Franklin was a well known American statesman, inventor, doctor and author. He had a reputation for testing new and unusual ideas, so most citizens of Philadelphia were not too surprised to see him trekking through the rain carrying a kite. In fact, many of them probably thought this was pretty mild behaviour considering the stories that had been told about him.

Take his famous dinner party. In 1750, so the story goes, Franklin hosted a Christmas dinner party for some close friends. Being a bit of a showman, he decided to astound them by using an electrical shock to kill the turkey they would be having for dinner. Little was known about electricity in those days, but that didn't stop Franklin. He had built a primitive battery system, one that could store large amounts of electricity for a period of time. His plan was to use the charged battery to electrocute the turkey.

All was ready. The guests had gathered. The batteries were charged. The unfortunate turkey waited nearby. Then Franklin made a mistake. He began to talk to one of the guests. Without thinking, he leaned against one of the batteries. A huge spark lit up the room as a jolt of electricity raced through his body. The shock knocked him to the floor.

After recovering, Franklin recalled the bang and spark of the discharge. How very much like lightning and thunder, he thought. Then his mind made an enormous leap: Could lightning be a huge jolt of electricity?

By the time a storm struck in June of 1752, Franklin was ready to find out. In a clearing he had walked to, he launched a kite. A metal spike fixed to the kite would attract electricity, if there was any, he figured. Attached to the lower end of the kite was twine, a weak conductor of electricity. And at the end of the twine was a silk ribbon, a non-conductor. Between the twine and the ribbon, Franklin fastened a key.

As he hoped, electrical charges collected on the spike and travelled down the string. When Franklin touched the key, there was a spark and a small jolt of electricity.

Franklin was lucky not to have been killed. In fact, he may not have known just how foolish —or how lucky! — he really was. When Russian scientist G.W. Richman tried to repeat Franklin's kite experiment his kite was struck by lightning and a 30-centimetre spark of electricity leaped from the ungrounded wire to his head, killing him in an instant!

Franklin's dangerous stunt proved what he had suspected. Lightning was indeed electricity. It also gave him another idea: If the key and spike could transmit electricity, maybe other conductors could do the same thing.

Franklin was so convinced of his findings that he ran a wire from the roof of his house to the ground. At one point lightning struck his roof, but was safely diverted through the wire to the ground. Franklin had created the lightning rod, a device we use to this day to protect buildings from lightning strikes.

More Extremes

- **Bell-ringing in Europe and England around Franklin's time was a hazardous activity. When storm clouds gathered, church bells would be rung violently in an effort to disrupt the lightning and to scare away evil spirits. Church steeples, however, were usually the highest points in town, so they often attracted lightning flashes. Records show that from 1753 to 1786, lightning struck 386 church towers in France alone and killed 103 bell ringers.**

5

• In the 1700s, gunpowder was often
stored in church vaults — a dangerous
practice considering the number of
lightning strikes churches suffered. In
1769 a lightning bolt struck the tower
of one church in Europe where 91
tonnes of gunpowder had been stored.
The explosion rocked the entire city,
levelling one-sixth of it and killing
3000 people. Once Franklin's lightning
rod was installed in churches, their
safety record greatly improved.

Dateline: Science
Understanding the Enemy

Snap your fingers. That probably took about a second to do. In that
same moment, lightning flashed at least a hundred times in different
places around the globe.

Lightning strikes can cause personal injury, even death. They
can also start forest fires, disrupt electrical services, fry computers,
knock out entire communication systems and disable aircraft.
Needless to say, lightning can be a powerful enemy. But knowing
and understanding the enemy can be the first step to victory. That's
why a dedicated bunch of modern scientists continue the work
started by Benjamin Franklin. Instead of kites and string, however,
they're using an arsenal of high-tech equipment to get close to the
action.

Most of that action is inside storm clouds. That's where charged
particles collect and separate, building up to enormous levels until
they discharge in a gigantic surge of electricity. To get close to the
action inside storm clouds, scientists resort to some clever methods.

One way is to fly close. Using high-altitude planes that travel at

700 kilometres per hour, scientists fly above approaching storm clouds. Then they take pictures of lightning and use sensitive equipment like computers, scanners and lasers to record information about electrical fields. More data is collected from space too. Videocameras in space shuttles capture images of lightning strikes that can be analyzed later.

Because no one knows exactly where or when a discharge will occur, scientists sometimes use rockets to trigger lightning strikes in a controlled way. When a thunderstorm appears on the horizon, small sounding rockets are launched into its centre. Attached to the rockets are long copper wires with electronic sensors near the end. When the rocket is struck by lighting, the wire is vaporized, and the sensor transmits information about the discharge to scientists below.

Extreme Facts

- You've likely heard the expression "as quick as lightning." That's fast. Lightning can jump from cloud to ground in 1/10,000 of a second, travelling at an amazing 100 000 kilometres per second. That's almost a million times faster than sound travels.
- There's power in lightning. If the energy from a single stroke of lightning could be harnessed, it could lift a mid-size car 100 kilometres into the air.
- At any given moment, there are 2000 thunderstorms occurring around the globe, producing an average of 100 flashes per second.
- A lightning flash is usually composed of four separate strokes or discharges.

Human Guinea Pig

Robert Chesebrough figured he had invented the perfect gel, a heal-all miracle spread guaranteed to soothe cuts and burns. Trouble was, he had to prove it . . . and the only guinea pig he had was himself.

Chesebrough, a twenty-six-year-old businessman, first stumbled upon his wonder gel while visiting the oilfields of Pennsylvania in 1863. He noticed one man scraping a black waxy substance from the machinery, then loading it into buckets to be hauled away.

"What is that stuff?" Chesebrough asked.

"Rod wax," the man answered. "Leftovers from the oil. It coats the pumps and slows them down. Got to get rid of it."

Chesebrough was about to turn away when the man continued, "The stuff's a nuisance, but the men sure love it. A little bit of this on a cut or scrape fixes it right up."

Suddenly interested, Chesebrough grabbed a bucket and filled it with rod wax. Maybe if he could get rid of the smell and the awful colour, he thought, the stuff had possibilities. After all, people were always on the lookout for quick-acting potions and salves.

At home Chesebrough started a series of experiments. Over the next ten years, he heated, mixed and processed the rod wax. In the end, he created the perfect formula — a clear, light-coloured, odourless gel.

But would it heal wounds and burns? There was only one way to find out. Test it. Find a subject with scrapes and cuts, apply the soothing salve, then wait and see. But where would he find someone with such an abundance of injuries?

Chesebrough decided to test the gel on himself. He inflicted dozens of cuts, bruises and burns to his body. Some he left untouched. Others he smothered in gel. When those wounds healed, he cut or burned himself some more. Before long his body looked like a patchwork quilt of injuries in various stages of repair.

The salve seemed to work. Wounds coated with it hurt less and healed faster. Would it work as well on other people? Chesebrough wondered. To find out, he stationed himself at construction sites, places guaranteed to provide a continuous flow of injuries. Sure enough, when workers hurt themselves Chesebrough was there, ready to apply his salve.

His subjects loved the gel. They claimed it soothed their pain and helped to heal wounds in record time. Convinced of its merits, Chesebrough bottled the gel and sold it to the public. Today Vaseline — the name he gave it — is still sold in grocery stores and pharmacies everywhere. As for Chesebrough, he claimed that daily doses of Vaseline gave him good health and long life. Perhaps it did. Chesebrough died a wealthy man in 1933, at the age of ninety-six.

Although today many newer ointments and salves for healing cuts and burns are available, Vaseline is still one of the most popular skin moisturizers around.

Being a guinea pig in your own medical experiments isn't exactly a wise practice, but Chesebrough wasn't the only person to do it.

• In 1953 Dr. Jonas Salk was on the brink of discovery. Across North America there had been an epidemic of polio, a disease that causes paralysis and even death. Salk had been working on a life-saving polio vaccine. With Salk's vaccine, people were injected with weak or dead polio germs in order to build up an immunity to the disease. But did the vaccine actually work, or would it, as some people feared, *infect* people with the disease instead?

Although there had already been

More EXtremes

widespread testing of the vaccine, Salk went a step further and injected it into himself before the final results were in. Fortunately the vaccine proved to be safe — and so effective that it has been used since then to save millions of lives.

• In 1979 Dr. Ryochi Naito of Japan tested a new blood product on himself. He had developed a blood substitute, an artificial substance derived from petroleum. If successful, the new product could be used in place of real blood in emergency transfusions. After many laboratory tests, Naito went one daring step further. He injected himself with 200 millilitres of the synthetic material to convince himself and others that the substance was safe and effective.

Explosive Mix

Alfred Nobel drew a deep breath and steadied his hands. He tried not to think of his dead brother, Emil, or of the demolished factory in Germany. Instead, he focused his attention on the vial of liquid before him. Carefully he let its contents drip into another container. Only after the vial was empty did he relax and breathe again.

Nobel had good reason to be nervous. The liquid was nitroglycerine, a highly unstable, very powerful explosive. A jiggle, a sudden bump, a slight change in temperature — that's all it took to set off an explosion.

The liquid had already taken its toll on the Nobel family. They owned several factories in Europe that manufactured explosives. Nitroglycerine was one of their most powerful explosives, but its unpredictable nature made it very dangerous to use. In 1864 an explosion had killed five workers, including Alfred's younger brother, Emil. Another explosion had destroyed a factory in Germany.

Alfred Nobel was determined to put an end to accidents such as these. In a laboratory in Sweden he conducted risky experiments, mixing nitroglycerine with other compounds, hoping to create a more durable yet still powerful explosive. For three years his attempts ended in failure. Sometimes the new mixtures were just as unstable as before. Other times they were too weak to be of any value.

One day in 1867 he made an interesting observation. Nitroglycerine from a broken flask had leaked into a clay-like packing material known as *kieselguhr*. The *kielselguhr* acted like a sponge, soaking up the nitroglycerine, but not reacting with it. The new compound was safe to handle, but when exploded it carried a force almost as powerful as nitroglycerine itself.

Nobel called the new explosive dynamite. With his discovery a powerful, dangerous liquid was transformed into an easy-to-use, safe solid.

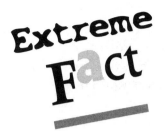

Extreme Fact

- Many people in Nobel's time were not aware of nitroglycerine's unpredictable nature. The liquid was sometimes for lamp oil, boot polish or as a lubricant on wagon wheels — often with deadly results.

Dateline: Science
Delivering the Best Punch

In a remote area, men and women wearing hard-hats scurry across a field. Behind they leave a tangle of cables, fuses, boxes of electronic wizardry and a strange cylinder. They race to a thick-walled concrete bunker that is partly buried into the side of a hill. Once they're inside, the door is closed and an alarm is sounded.

A siren blares. One of them punches a button, shooting thousands of volts of electricity along the cable. In an instant there's a flash of light, a dull thud and a cloud of smoke. When the dust settles, the team emerges. Just as they hoped, the cylinder is a mangled mess . . .

The people in hard-hats are scientists. This is the laboratory where they do research into explosives. And inside the cylinder are several black, greasy stones — industrial diamonds that they have just created.

Explosions can cause destruction, but they have constructive uses too. Producing cheap industrial-grade diamonds on demand is one of them. Joining metals together is another. They're also used for construction, mining, fireworks and propelling rockets into space. Carefully placed explosives are even used to extinguish burning oil well fires. The powerful blast literally blows out the fire.

There are over 20 000 different kinds of explosives. Most are chemical explosives, close relatives to dynamite and gunpowder. When they are detonated, a chemical reaction occurs. A large amount of heat and rapidly expanding gas is produced in a fraction of a second. The expanding gas shoots shock waves through the air and ground, smashing large objects into smaller pieces, sealing one metal to another, or beginning a chain of other reactions.

It is the explosion scientist's job to discover new uses for explosives, and new ways of delivering the greatest punch in the safest and most efficient manner possible.

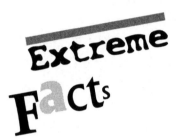

Extreme Facts

- **Chemical explosions take just a few millionths of a second to start, but they create massive energy at terrific speeds. Their earth-shattering waves race through the ground at more than 3000 metres per second.**
- **Nuclear explosives are much more powerful than chemical explosives. A ball of uranium small enough to fit in your hand can be made to explode with a force equal to over 18 000 tonnes of dynamite.**
- **The world's strongest explosions are not chemical or nuclear. They're volcanic. The sudden eruption of a volcano can be many times more forceful than any human-made explosive. In 1883 a volcano on the island of Krakatoa in Indonesia erupted with a force twenty-six times greater than any atomic bomb ever tested, making it the largest explosion ever recorded on our planet.**

Locked in Ice

Norwegian scientist Fridtjof Nansen was fascinated by a report about a ship that had sunk off the coast of Siberia, then had mysteriously turned up three years later near Greenland, over 3000 kilometres away. How was it possible for a wreck locked in Arctic ice to travel such a distance? Nansen asked himself. His answer: ocean currents. Powerful currents under the surface ice must have slowly carried the ship northward.

Nansen hatched a wild scheme to prove his theory. Why not build a special ship — a sturdy, uncrushable ship — sail it to the Arctic, freeze it in the ice, then simply let it drift? Let the currents, if they existed, drag the ship on its course. But in order to take precise measurements and map the ship's route, Nansen would have to be aboard it . . . possibly for up to five years in the frozen Arctic.

Excited rather than frightened by the idea, Nansen approached the Norwegian government for funding, and started building a vessel sturdy enough to withstand the crushing pressure of the Arctic ice. The *Fram*, as the ship was called, was a short, broad vessel with thick sides reinforced by beams and braces. Its hull was curved and rounded so that when ice closed in around it, the pressure would lift the ship out of the water rather than smash it.

On June 24, 1893, the *Fram* set off from Norway carrying a crew of thirteen men and enough supplies to last two to five years. It headed along the coast of Russia, where it stopped briefly to take thirty-four Siberian sled dogs on board. Then it veered sharply north. In September the crew spotted ice floes. Nansen steered into the midst of the floes, shut off the engines . . . and waited.

Weeks later it happened. The crew was below deck when suddenly a deafening noise echoed through the ship. At that moment huge slabs of ice shifted, collided, rose up on one another and started to lock and freeze together into a giant mass. The heaving ice squeezed the *Fram*. It trembled, pitched and rolled. But as planned, the ship was not crushed. Instead the ice pushed it up, and when the pressure passed the *Fram* slowly sank back down, half above and half below the ice surface.

Months passed. The crew took weather readings, measured the ocean's temperature and depth, dredged up samples from the bottom, and plotted the ship's movement.

The measurements pointed out a disturbing fact. The ice was moving more slowly than Nansen expected. And the ship was off course. The voyage that Nansen expected would take two to five years looked as if it might last seven or eight! Even then the ship might not reach the North Pole as planned.

As the expedition headed into its third winter, Nansen came up with a daring plan for rescue. On March 14, 1895, he left the ship with a sledge, a team of dogs and one companion, Hjalmar Johansen. Nansen hoped to travel overland to the North Pole and beyond, something no human had done before. With luck he would encounter people who might be able to rescue *Fram's* desperate crew.

Nansen figured the trip would take a few weeks. But navigational errors threw the two men off course, and as summer arrived the ice broke up, making travel even more difficult and dangerous. The two men took shelter on a small island. Without food, they were forced to kill most of their dogs . . . and keep waiting.

Nansen and his companion spent the next winter, their third in the snowbound north, huddled in a small hut. The following spring their luck changed. Hearing dogs barking, Nansen followed the sound. He met a stranger who turned out to be a British explorer, Frederick Jackson, who was on an expedition to discover a new land route to the North Pole.

Nansen and Johansen sailed back to Norway in the British ship. On August 20, 1896, a week after their arrival, the *Fram* turned up too — three years and three months after its departure from Norway. For almost three years it had been locked in ice, floating westward, until warmer weather finally freed it from its icy grip. Nansen's daring experiment proved that his hunch was correct after all. Just as he had predicted, the *Fram* had continued to drift, drawn by a mysterious polar current.

More EXtremes

• Although most ships don't venture into polar seas the way the *Fram* did, Arctic ice can be a formidable enemy even for ships travelling farther south. As everyone who has heard about the *Titanic* knows, icebergs can sink even the largest of vessels.

More Extremes

- Icebergs are made from Arctic snow that never melted. They are formed in a process known as "calving," in which large chunks of ice break off from glaciers or ice sheets and tumble into the sea.

- The most dangerous iceberg region lies just off the eastern coast of Newfoundland, in a well travelled area known as Iceberg Alley. Most icebergs here get their start in Greenland. Although about 10 000 icebergs are calved each year, only an average of 466 make it to Newfoundland. Most melt before getting that far south.

- Only about one-eighth of an iceberg is visible. The rest is hidden below water.

- How big can an iceberg be? The famous *Titanic* iceberg was about 18 metres across at the water line, but the record holder for an Arctic iceberg is one spotted in 1882 — 11 kilometres long and 6 wide.

- Icebergs form in Antarctica too. Antarctic icebergs are typically bigger than Arctic ones. The largest Antarctic iceberg on record was a 1956 monster nearly 300 kilometres long and 100 kilometres wide.

Killer . . . or Cure?

When Marie Curie first noticed the painful red sores on her fingers, she was disturbed. Then she became interested in what might have caused them. So did her husband, Pierre.

Marie and Pierre Curie were scientists who worked with radioactive substances in the late 1800s. They were especially interested in pitchblende, a black mineral ore that contained radioactive elements the Curies were trying to isolate and identify. This meant years of slaving over hot fires in their laboratory inside an abandoned wooden shed on the grounds of a Paris university, boiling tonnes of pitchblende, extracting, filtering and purifying one batch of crystals after another. Here Pierre Curie conducted delicate tests on the refined crystals. Marie, meanwhile, worked in the yard, stoking the fires, stirring large cast-iron pots of pitchblende and pouring the mixtures from one container to another.

Constant exposure to pitchblende produced the red sores on Marie's fingers, making it painful for her to handle equipment. Pierre worried about her health. After several weeks, however, the sores slowly disappeared on their own, and the Curies' concern shifted to fascination.

Radiation from pitchblende, it seemed, killed cells. That would explain the red sores on Marie's fingers. In time, however, the sores disappeared. Somehow, given time to heal, healthy cells had replaced the dead ones. Did radiation always have this effect? Would it always kill cells, then allow new ones to take their place? Would it always work on diseased cells in the same way? Would radiation, for example, kill cancer cells, allowing healthy ones to take their place? What a medical miracle that would be!

To test their ideas, the Curies first needed to identify and isolate the radioactive substances in pitchblende. One night in September, 1902, the Curies went home, exhausted from their long day, but convinced that they were very close to a breakthrough. They had poured the last batch of purified pitchblende crystals into small glass bowls, leaving them on tables and shelves that lined the laboratory. As they were about to go to sleep, Marie convinced Pierre to return to the laboratory. Some unknown force, she said, beckoned her.

The Curies let themselves into the darkened shed and moved cautiously between the rows of tables. A strange bluish-purple glow from 6000 glass bowls created an unwavering soft light that filled the room.

The crystals turned out to be a new radioactive element — radium. Pierre wasted no time testing its medical powers. He deliberately exposed his own arm to the rays. As he hoped, a burn appeared. But within eight weeks it disappeared, leaving little more than a tiny grey mark on his arm. Pierre repeated the experiment on animals, with the same results. Exposure to radium killed living cells. But when the exposure was over, healthy cells grew in their place.

Other scientists continued the work started by the Curies. Their experiments showed that carefully controlled doses of radiation could be used to kill diseased cells like cancer, giving the body a chance to make new cells to replace them. In time, radium became an accepted cancer-fighting weapon.

The Curies received a Nobel prize for their discovery, but their work was cut short by tragedy. In April, 1906, Pierre was knocked down and killed by a horse-drawn wagon on a Paris street. Marie died on July 4, 1934. Her constant exposure to radiation over the years had left her body weakened and susceptible to disease. She died of the very thing she sought to cure — cancer.

Extreme

Fact**s**

- **The Curies' daughter, Irène, and her husband, Frédéric Joliot, won the Nobel Prize for chemistry in 1935 for their discovery of artificial radioactivity.**
- **Even today, the note pages left by the Curies give off powerful doses of radiation.**

An Explosive Pile

Scientists sometimes take huge risks to run an experiment. And sometimes they put others in danger too. On December 2, 1942, most people in Chicago went about their usual business, unaware that under a nearby football field a grand experiment was underway — one that could blow up half of their city if it went awry.

The experiment was the brainchild of an Italian-born physicist, Enrico Fermi. Fermi had a great interest in nuclear fission, a reaction in which atoms are split. Was there some way to harness this energy? he wondered.

So did the American government. In 1942 most of the world was at war, and the United States was looking for a way to stop Germany's deadly march across Europe. Perhaps nuclear fission was the solution: Tap into the power of the atom, channel its hidden energy, conquer the enemy. That became the government plan. But how to do it?

With funding from the U.S. government, Fermi continued his research. In fission, tiny particles are fired at atoms, splitting them, knocking out more particles and releasing heat and light. If a single split atom released a small amount of energy, thousands of atoms combined together would release much more. Was it possible to set up a chain of reactions, Fermi wondered, with each reaction building on the energy released by the others?

Fermi believed it was possible. Fission not only released energy from an atom, it also whacked a tiny particle known as a neutron out of the atom's core. If that neutron could be steered toward another atom, it might smash it too, releasing more energy and another neutron to continue the process. Neutron by neutron, atom by split atom, the reaction could continue, building energy to tremendous levels.

In an abandoned squash court under Stagg Field at the University of Chicago, Fermi built a reactor to do the job. He and his fellow scientists piled 360 tonnes of graphite bricks in layers, staggering the bricks to allow spaces in between. Some of the bricks contained pellets of uranium, a rich source of neutrons. The uranium would fuel the reaction; the graphite would slow down the neutrons to just the right splitting speed. As a safety feature, cadmium rods — a neutron-absorbing material — were inserted among the bricks. By adding or removing the rods, Fermi hoped to keep the speed of the reaction in check.

Building the reactor was a messy job. As soon as the blocks started going into place, the floor of the squash court became black with graphite. Scientists slipped and slithered on the greasy surface as they piled one brick on another. By the morning of December 2, 1942, the reactor was finished. Fermi gave the order to begin the experiment. Still, no one in the stadium above knew of the danger right below their feet.

Anxiously the crew watched as the cadmium rods were removed. Little by little, radiation counters began to click, indicating that the reaction had started. By noon a hush had fallen over the room. Spectators grew more tense as the last rod was pulled — a few centimetres at a time — from the bricks, and radiation levels shot higher. But the spectators weren't as tense as the three men perched on top of the reactor. The three, called the suicide squad, were armed only with buckets of cadmium solution in case the reaction went horribly sour. If they didn't have enough cadmium to slow the reaction . . .

By 3:25 p.m. the chain reaction was in full swing and the experiment was a success. As the reactor operated, firing neutrons, splitting atoms and releasing energy — all of it under the tight supervision of Enrico Fermi — most Chicagoans were still blissfully unaware of the danger to their city. Even fewer knew that the world had slipped into the nuclear age.

More EXtremes

• On July 16, 1945, Dr. Robert Bacher witnessed first-hand the awesome power of the atom through a nerve-wracking experience of his own. Along with Enrico Fermi and other nuclear scientists from around the United States, Bacher came to a lonely desert in New Mexico to set off the world's first atomic bomb. Bacher's job was to arm the weapon by inserting a radioactive core into the giant bomb before it was hoisted to the top of a tall steel tower.

The procedure did not go well. The extreme desert heat expanded the core, making the fit difficult. Then a thunderstorm struck. An old army tent was tossed over the bomb and Bacher and several others took refuge under it. With lightning flashing around the steel tower, the scientists sat huddled around the most devastating device ever created, aware that one wayward stroke of lightning would put an explosive end to their experiment . . . and them. Eventually the storm passed and the test went ahead as planned. The bomb was detonated, sending a mushroom cloud over the desert. The nuclear age, for good or bad, was here to stay.

Cast Adrift . . . on Purpose

"I have had enough," Alain Bombard scrawled in his log after a month of battling storms, sharks and starvation.

Bombard was in the middle of the Atlantic. He had spent forty days alone in a flimsy rubber dinghy. He had lost weight. His body was dehydrated and covered with festering sores. He hadn't slept for days. Thoroughly exhausted, he wrote his will and prepared to die. Astonishingly, Alain Bombard hadn't ended up on the dinghy by accident. He had purposely cast himself adrift on the ocean.

Bombard was a young French doctor who worked in a hospital near the Atlantic coast. Often he was called to tend shipwreck victims. He was surprised to learn that many people who made it to lifeboats still died within three days at sea. He felt that more castaways would survive if only they knew more about the ocean and its abundant resources. To prove his point, he planned a dangerous experiment. Alone and with only meagre supplies, he would cross the Atlantic in a rubber dinghy, relying solely upon the ocean for his survival.

In October, 1952, Bombard cast himself into the Atlantic Ocean. He took no food, water or fishing equipment. He would try to survive on the same terms as shipwreck survivors did.

He speared fish with a homemade harpoon. Using their bones, he made crude hooks. With this primitive equipment he caught many more fish, his main source of food. To balance his diet, he scooped tiny plankton from the water. But the biggest problem for castaways is not lack of food. It is fresh water. Drinking salt water from the ocean dehydrates the body, increasing thirst and eventually leading to death if the practice is continued. To satisfy his need for fresh water, Bombard cut slits in the sides of fish he caught, and sucked out their juice. It was barely enough liquid to survive.

With over 6000 kilometres of ocean to cross, Bombard knew he had to stick to a rigid routine. He woke at dawn, ate at precise times, exercised daily, conducted frequent inspections of his dinghy, wrote in his log and relaxed by reading books.

Days turned into weeks. By night Bombard froze; by day he baked. His body became coated with salt from the ocean spray. Ferocious storms almost swamped the boat, leaving him wet and shivering. One time a shark attacked his dinghy, terrifying him until it finally lost interest and left. But his worst problems were caused by his own lack of sailing experience. Bombard had trouble using his sextant for navigating, and unknowingly drifted far off course.

On December 6, his health deteriorating and his spirit broken, Bombard wrote his will. Three days later he spotted a British cargo ship on the horizon. He signalled the crew and was soon on board, enjoying a refreshing shower and a satisfying meal. But he knew he couldn't stay. Only a complete voyage across the ocean would prove that his ideas were right. Despite objections from the crew, Bombard reboarded the dinghy to continue on his way.

But now he encountered another problem. His rubber dinghy began to deteriorate, allowing water to seep through the bottom. He spent most of his time bailing to stay afloat. Finally, on the evening of December 20, he spotted a flashing light in the distance. By dawn the coastline of Barbados was visible. After sixty-five days at sea, Bombard's journey was over.

Armed with the simplest of supplies, he had succeeded in crossing the Atlantic in a rubber dinghy. He proved that the ocean could sustain the lives of those who were skilled in using its abundant resources.

Swamped and Sinking

Almost two decades later, another scientist ventured across the ocean for an entirely different reason . . . and he too almost lost his life on the voyage.

Thor Heyerdahl was in the middle of the ocean, far from any land, when a massive wave battered his ship from behind, tipping it, swamping its deck, and snapping a main steering oar to pieces. The ship began to sink.

Heyerdahl was no ordinary man and his ship, Ra II, no commonplace vessel. Heyerdahl was an anthropologist, keen to prove that ancient people could have journeyed across the Atlantic long before Christopher Columbus. To prove his theory he had Ra II built to resemble ships used by Egyptians three thousand years ago. No screws, nails or bolts held Ra II together. No motor powered it. Made of almost 7 tonnes of papyrus reeds lashed together with rope, equipped with sails and wooden oars, topped with a rickety cabin the size of a garden shed, the vessel was short, flat and wide.

Many thought Heyerdahl was crazy. Even modern ships could run into trouble crossing the Atlantic. Ra II faced greater challenges. Because papyrus soaks up water, many people predicted it would become waterlogged and sink after less than two weeks on the open seas. Its flat shape would make it difficult to steer too. Without a motor it would be at the mercy of prevailing winds and currents.

Heyerdahl brushed such criticisms aside and gathered a crew of eight scientists, journalists and sailors. To make the voyage as authentic as possible, only foods preserved in the manner of the ancient Egyptians were loaded on board: dried and salted meat and fish, dates, figs, flour, oil and Egyptian bread. Water was carried in goatskin bags and jars. In place of modern navigational equipment, the men would rely on the stars to guide them across the ocean.

On May 17, 1970, Ra II set sail from the coast of Africa. From the start, the voyage was anything but smooth. The reeds, as predicted, soaked up water, becoming heavier and causing the ship to sink dangerously low in the water. Days of calm left the ship at a standstill. Then treacherous winds and storms tossed the vessel so violently that the crew and their belongings were almost pitched overboard. The greatest threat, however, struck mid-way through the voyage.

When the huge wave hit, it crippled the ship. Water swept over *Ra II*, filling its middle section and plunging it even deeper into the water. With its steering oar broken, the ship turned sideways and became impossible to control. *Ra II* dipped and rolled, slammed by waves, stranded and helpless, thousands of kilometres from land.

The crew acted quickly. Lopping off chunks of reeds from the higher ends of the ship, they stuffed the cavity in the centre so that water could not fill it further. By lashing broken bits of the steering shaft together, they made a rough replacement for the original. Then the main mast was moved forward, allowing the sail to catch the wind and making steering easier.

With these makeshift improvements *Ra II* carried on, slowly plowing its way through choppy seas. Days became weeks. Then on the fifty-seventh day a sweet smell wafted over the ship, the familiar scent of green grass. A few hours later *Ra II* steered into the harbour of Bridgetown, Barbados, her mission complete, her voyage a success.

Aboard a primitive ship, using centuries-old sailing methods and tools, Thor Heyerdahl had proved his point in an astonishing way. A papyrus ship could cross a major ocean. Ancient people might have visited the Americas long before the time of Christopher Columbus.

• *Ra II* wasn't Thor Heyerdahl's first ocean-crossing experiment. In 1947 he built a balsa raft named the *Kon-Tiki*. With five companions he sailed across 8000 kilometres of ocean to prove that ancient South Americans could have travelled to the islands of Polynesia thousands of years ago.

Surrounded by Sharks

Do you have to be crazy to swim with sharks? They can rip prey to pieces in seconds, yet marine scientist Eugenie Clark regularly swims with them. One of her greatest thrills, however, came from a more innocent-looking fish not much bigger than your two hands.

In 1960, while diving in the Red Sea, Clark netted a small fish known as a Moses sole. She was surprised to see milky fluid oozing from the pores near its fins. When Clark touched it, her fingers tingled and stiffened. I've been poisoned, she thought.

The dose had been small and harmless, but it aroused Clark's curiosity. In 1972 she began a series of experiments to discover more about the Moses sole. She put the small fish in a large plastic bag along with other fish. Through the sides of the bag she squeezed the Moses sole, forcing a few drops of white fluid into the water. In minutes every other fish in the bag was dead.

What effect would the Moses sole have on larger fish? Clark wondered. She put one in the same tank as several sharks. The sharks lunged at the small fish, then suddenly jerked away, rolled from side to side and leaped about the tank. The Moses sole continued swimming as if nothing had happened. But when Clark washed the skin of the sole with alcohol to remove any traces of the sticky fluid, the sharks devoured it in seconds.

How would sharks in the wild behave when they encountered the Moses sole? To find out, Clark and her assistants baited a line with different kinds of fish, some alive, others dead. Between the fish they attached the Moses sole. They dropped the line into shark-infested waters, donned scuba gear and plunged into the sea to watch. Sharks swarmed around the swimmers, dodging them, intent on gobbling the bait. In a wild frenzy they ripped all the fish from the line. All except one kind — the Moses sole.

Clark's experiments showed that even tiny traces of the Moses sole's white fluid sent sharks scrambling for safety. The poison had long-lasting effects too. A spoonful of the chemical kept the hungriest of sharks away for up to eighteen hours.

Because of Clark's discovery, the future for divers looks bright. Manufactured into a lotion and applied to diving suits, the poison of the Moses sole may be one of the most effective shark repellents ever found.

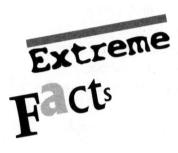

Extreme Facts

- **A Moses sole has about 240 poison glands, each one secreting milky fluid through tiny pores in its skin.**
- **The poison works quickly. In seconds it attacks the victim's nervous system and destroys red blood cells, causing convulsions and hemorrhaging.**
- **Dangerous as it is, the Moses sole is quite tasty. Local people along the Red Sea eat the fish once they have cooked it to neutralize its poison.**
- **Another shark researcher experimented with her own version of shark protection. In 1980 Valerie Taylor wore a steel-mesh suit similar to the chain mail worn by medieval knights, and plunged into shark-infested waters. Attracted by the bait she carried, a blue shark lunged at Taylor, sinking its teeth into her arm. The good news was, the suit worked: the shark's teeth never made it through the steel mesh. But the bulky suit added 7 kilograms of weight to Taylor, making escape slow and awkward.**

Changing Poison into Medicine

Some people milk cows or goats. Charles Kristensen milks spiders. Poisonous ones like tarantulas and black widows.

Kristensen is an arachnologist, a scientist who studies spiders. Since 1980 he's been doing what others haven't dared to do — extracting the venom from spiders. In fact, he keeps over 40 000 of them in cups, buckets and pails around his home, just for this purpose.

To "milk" a spider, Kristensen holds it with a pair of tweezers and inserts a needle into its mouth. Then he taps a foot pedal, sending a mild electrical charge to the needle. The charge stimulates the spider, causing it to release a tiny bead of venom. Using a fine dropper, Kristensen sucks up the venom, then returns the spider, unharmed, to its former home.

Depending upon the spider, it may take anywhere from one to a thousand milkings to produce a single drop of venom, but Kristensen is a patient man who understands the importance of his work. Spider venom, like the venom from snakes, scorpions, bees, slugs and even snails, is a prized commodity in the world of science. Researchers have found that venom contains dozens of toxins, each one having its own special properties. And while venom can kill, its toxins may also heal and protect when properly used.

Take the case of the copperhead snake, a relative of the rattlesnake. A bite from this pinkish brown snake injects a quick-acting poison that attacks the blood. But scientists have discovered that the poison can have useful properties too. A protein extracted from the venom of the copperhead shrinks certain types of cancer tumours. Integrilin, found in the venom of a rattlesnake, can be used to treat people suffering from chest pains and minor heart attacks. Dendrotoxins, found in the venom of such dangerous snakes as the deadly mamba, show promise in the fight against Alzheimer's disease and epilepsy. Another toxin found in some spider venoms blocks nerve cells and may one day be useful in controlling strokes and seizures.

The study of venoms can be useful in other ways too. By examining the chemical makeup of the poison, scientists develop antevenom serums. These counteract the effects of the toxins and can be used to save anyone who has been bitten by the poisonous creature.

As more is discovered about the usefulness of venom, the work of daring people like Charles Kristensen could save thousands of lives.

2

EXtreme Tests and Demonstrations

Trying the untried . . . testing the untested

An inventor fails 999 times, and if he succeeds, he is in. He treats his failures as practice shots.

Charles Kettering

Arnie Mangold has been shot more than 150 times. He claims it doesn't hurt a bit.

Mangold works for Foster-Miller Inc., a company that has invented a new criminal-stopping device called the Snare-Net. In these tests, Mangold positions himself about six metres from a grenade launcher. The launcher fires a canister packed with a huge plastic net. Two metres from the launch site, the net opens and spreads out like a billowing parachute, swallowing Mangold. No matter how hard he struggles, he quickly becomes entangled.

The net could help police stop criminals in a safe and harmless way, Mangold believes. After all, it works on him, doesn't it?

Tests and demonstrations are an important part of proving the worth of new ideas and products. Tests point out strengths and weaknesses. By knowing what works and what doesn't, researchers can make adjustments and improvements. Demonstrations serve another purpose. Going public — showing just how useful and successful an idea or product can be — is a way of getting others to support your project or invention.

Tests and demonstrations can often be routine. Sometimes, though, they can be dramatic, bold, even risky. Like Mangold and the Snare-Net, they can be extreme.

The King Disappears!

Murmurs of concern rippled among the spectators that lined the River Thames in London, England. The boat that had been floating gracefully had started sinking — with King James himself on board!

The crowd needn't have worried. The boat was no ordinary vessel. It was the clever invention of Cornelis Drebbel, a Dutchman, and its journey down the Thames in 1620 was no leisurely cruise. It was a daring demonstration involving the King of England himself.

Drebbel had designed an unusual water craft which he called a "diving boat." Although it was made of wood like other boats of its time, Drebbel's vessel was wrapped in greased leather, making it fully enclosed and airtight. Oars extended through the sides, sealed with tight-fitting leather flaps to prevent water from leaking in. The boat was large enough to hold twelve oarsmen and several passengers, and was outfitted with two other unusual features: a series of large leather bags strapped to the hull, and a set of air hoses that extended above the boat. With these, Drebbel's vessel could do something no other boat could do — sink below the water, then bob back to the surface.

When the boat was afloat, the leather bags were flat and stoppered, the air squeezed completely out of them. At a moment's notice, however, Drebbel could open the bags, allowing water to gush inside, adding weight to the boat, and forcing it to sink beneath the surface. Air hoses attached to floats rose to the surface, providing the men on board with oxygen. By squeezing the water out of the bags, Drebbel could reverse the process, making the boat lighter and causing it to rise again.

The daring demonstration worked. The boat sank four metres, travelled for over 10 kilometres underwater, then rose gracefully back to the surface. The entire journey took three hours. At the end, King James emerged safe and sound to declare that the world's first submarine was a great success.

- **Drebbel also designed and built microscopes, telescopes, thermostats, incubators, toys and clocks. He discovered a way of making oxygen, using chemicals. It is possible that he used this process to replace the air hoses in submarines he later constructed.**
- **Some of Drebbel's contemporaries actually thought he was a sorcerer, but today his work is so admired by scientists and inventors that a crater on the moon has been named after him. The Drebbel Lunar Crater measures 30 kilometres in diameter.**

Dazzling the Emperor

In 1654, in a courtyard before the emperor of the Holy Roman Empire and his lords and ladies, Otto von Guericke took two copper bowls, greased their edges and carefully fitted them together to form a sphere. He held it up for all to see, then with a simple tug he pulled the two bowls apart.

The emperor fidgeted impatiently. Why was von Guericke wasting time on such antics?

But von Guericke was hardly finished. Taking the same two bowls, he fitted them together once more. This time he attached a special pump he had invented, and sucked the air from the sphere to create a vacuum inside. Then he attached two horses to each side of the sphere and gave the order to begin pulling. Whips snapped. The horses lurched, straining on the harnesses. The bowls that had separated so easily before, now held. The emperor leaned forward, suddenly interested.

Next von Guericke added two more horses to each end. Still the seal could not be broken. Horse after horse was added, each pulling and straining with all its might. It wasn't until sixteen horses, eight pulling from each side, were added that the sphere finally separated. The audience burst into applause. Otto von Guericke's elaborate demonstration had convinced the audience of a scientific truth more effectively than words ever could.

Air pressure is impressive stuff. Properly used it can create a bond so tight, so strong, that even the most powerful forces would have difficulty breaking it apart.

Sealed and Submerged

You are being sealed inside an airtight wooden tube the size of a coffin. It's a tight fit and the only light entering the tube comes from a small glass window near your face. By squirming a bit, you locate holes in the tube on either side of your body. You jam your arms into them and feel the rush of cool air on your skin as they stick outside. Suddenly you feel the tube being raised and then lowered. You try not to panic as darkness engulfs your tiny window, water swirls around your arms, and you realize that you are being swallowed by the sea . . .

That's how John Lethbridge might have felt the first time he tried his unusual invention. Lethbridge was an eighteenth century British inventor who had a passion for underwater diving. Like other divers of his time, though, he could only descend a few metres below the surface, and he could only stay submerged for as long as he could hold his breath. But Lethbridge wanted to dive deeper for longer periods. To do the job, he invented the world's first diving suit.

Lethbridge's invention actually looked more like a wooden barrel than a suit of clothes. It was a long tapered tube made out of sturdy oak, with a single glass porthole at one end. To use it, Lethbridge crawled inside and lay down flat. He stuck his arms through special sealed holes in the side. Then the contraption was lowered into water and compressed air was fed into it through long tubes connected to the surface.

Lethbridge called the strange device a diving engine. He demonstrated it for the first time in 1715 and used it many times afterwards. With his invention, he could stay submerged for thirty minutes at a time and reach depths of 18 metres — feats unheard of before his invention. Because his arms were free to move, Lethbridge could handle tools and equipment under water, making the diving engine a useful tool for recovering salvage from sunken ships.

Extreme Fact

• Sabotage was the reason for Jacques-Yves Cousteau's improvement on the diving suit. A French scientist and inventor, Cousteau was also part of the French Resistance in the Second World War, determined to rid the ocean of German ships. Traditional diving equipment was too bulky and awkward to use without being detected by the enemy, so in 1943 Cousteau invented a portable breathing apparatus. To prove that it worked, he strapped on the device and repeatedly plunged into the sea, making each dive deeper than the one before. His invention, the aqualung, revolutionized undersea exploration, allowing divers freedom to swim undetected and untethered.

Falling from the Sky

As a war prisoner, Frenchman André-Jacques Garnerin had time on his hands. Time to plot his escape. He thought of breaking down the door to his prison, of overpowering his guards, and a dozen other schemes. But his wildest idea was to leap from the window of his prison tower and drift to the ground holding an umbrella-like device.

Garnerin was still hatching this scheme when he was released from prison, and he never forgot it. Instead, he built it. He made a

7-metre canopy from white canvas and attached it to a small wicker basket. Then he planned an incredibly dangerous demonstration.

On October 22, 1797, in front of a crowd of spectators, Garnerin inflated a large hydrogen balloon and hooked the canopy to it. The balloon rose into the air, carrying Garnerin in the basket that hung below. At 1000 metres he cut the cord connecting the basket to the balloon. The balloon shot skyward. Garnerin plunged to the ground like a stone. Then as his canvas canopy filled with air, it billowed out, slowing his fall.

Garnerin was thrilled. So was the crowd below. But then, quite unexpectedly, the canopy began to sway back and forth as air trapped in it spilled from the edges. At first the motion was gentle and soothing, but as more air gushed from the canopy, its pace quickened, sending it careening wildly from side to side. Nausea swept over Garnerin. He hung on, praying for a quick end to his adventure. When he finally reached the ground, he blacked out.

Garnerin later improved the design of his parachute. He added a vent hole at the top of the canopy so that trapped air streamed through the opening, keeping the parachute on a straight and stable path. Then he made more jumps, each one higher and more daring than the one before.

• Garnerin wasn't the only family member with high-flying interests. In 1858 his daughter, Eliza, made the leap, too, becoming the first woman to parachute from a high-altitude balloon.

"Cut the rope!"

As a crowd of spectators gathered, a bearded man mounted a platform at the New York Exposition in 1853. An assistant pulled a rope and the platform rose, a little at first, then gradually higher and higher until it hung in mid-air high above the crowd. The bearded man waited until all eyes were upon him, then he barked an order.

"Cut the rope!"

The crowd gasped, certain that the platform would crash to the ground, injuring or perhaps killing the man on board. Instead, the platform jerked briefly, then stopped. The man bowed and smiled as the crowd broke into applause.

That man was Elisha Otis, a daredevil inventor. Otis had arranged this stunt to convince others of the worth of his latest invention, the safety elevator.

In the 1800s elevators were raised and lowered by ropes and pulleys. Often the ropes frayed and broke, causing serious injuries for anyone in the elevator if it fell. Otis devised a clever system to prevent such accidents. He attached a heavy coiled spring to the moving platform. As long as the rope supporting the platform remained taut, the spring stayed tightly coiled. The moment the rope failed, however, the spring uncoiled, pressing metal teeth outward from the platform to catch onto notched side rails. Once the teeth engaged the side rails, the platform was brought to a sudden stop.

Otis's demonstration dazzled the crowds and convinced builders that his invention was safe. In 1857 the first Otis elevator was installed in a New York hotel. By 1868 office buildings were using Otis safety elevators, too.

The safety elevator totally changed the world of construction. Buildings grew from five storeys (all the stairs people could comfortably climb) to ten, twelve, even more storeys. Elisha Otis's simple device ushered in the age of skyscrapers, enabling builders to fit more buildings and more people into the same ground space as before. Today's modern cities look the way they do, thanks in part to the elevator.

Extreme Facts

- **One in every four elevators worldwide bears the Otis name. Of the hundred tallest buildings in the world, sixty have Otis high-rise equipment.**
- **What is the safest form of transportation? If you thought trains, planes or automobiles, think again. Elevators are not only the safest form of transportation, they also accumulate more distance in one year than all other kinds.**
- **Many of today's elevators move at speeds up to 33 kilometres per hour. People travelling in these express elevators sometimes suffer from popping of the ears, which can occur at speeds above 16 kilometres per hour.**
- **The world's fastest elevator is in Japan's Landmark Hotel in Yokohama. It will take you up to the sixty-ninth floor in 40 seconds at an ear-popping speed of 45 kilometres per hour.**

• The elevators in the CN Tower —
the world's tallest free-standing
structure — travel at a good speed
too: 22 kilometres per hour.

In the Nick of Time

In September of 1868, a steam locomotive chugged along the rails in a Pittsburgh train yard, its speed building slowly to 50 kilometres per hour. From the train, George Westinghouse, inventor and businessman, watched intently. So did others who had been invited to attend.

Westinghouse wanted to show people his new compression brakes for trains, so he organized a daring demonstration. But Westinghouse might not have known just how daring the demonstration would become. Maybe it was planned, maybe it was accidental. Either way, nothing could have shown off Westinghouse's new invention in a more extreme way.

Suddenly a horse-driven wagon darted in front of the speeding train and stalled on the tracks. In panic, the driver whipped the horses. They reared, tossing the driver off the cart and onto the tracks. Quickly the engineer turned a brake handle. The wheels locked. The train slid along the rails, wheels screeching, the huge weight skidding closer and closer to the wagon and its driver.

Aboard the train, people held their breath. A train this size, going this speed, would never be able to stop in time. But this was no ordinary train. This train was equipped with Westinghouse's latest invention, air brakes. The moment the brake handle was turned, compressed air pushed the brakes against the train wheels. The train slowed to a stop, just an arm's length from the grateful driver.

Up until this time, trains were equipped with friction brakes. Brakemen on the trains had to turn separate hand wheels in each car of the train — a process that was slow and ineffective. Trains often failed to stop in time, colliding with each other or skidding off the rails, with disastrous results.

George Westinghouse's air brakes were much more effective. A tank under the locomotive held compressed air. The moment the engineer turned the brake handle, valves released the air, sending it along pipes to each car of the train. Just fifteen years after the Pittsburgh demonstration, over 50 000 train cars were equipped with Westinghouse's air brakes to make their stops quicker, smoother and safer.

Dateline: Science
Shooting to Improve

What does it take to stop one object from hitting and demolishing another? In Westinghouse's case it was air brakes to stop a train from smashing into a cart and driver. But sometimes it's not a train that's dangerous, but flying garbage! In high-impact research, guns and cannons are actually used to make our world safer.

Deadly Garbage

One of the greatest dangers in space comes from the garbage that orbits earth. Nuts, bolts, paint chips — rubbish and cast-offs from forty years of space travel — rip around the planet at 16 kilometres per second. A large chunk of debris can bring an entire mission to a disastrous end if it plows into a spacecraft that crosses its path. Even the tiniest piece of space junk can cause major damage. In 1983 a paint chip rammed into the space shuttle *Challenger*, gouging a small crater out of one of its windows.

That's where the Whipple shield and engineers at the Johnson Space Center in Houston, Texas, come in handy. A Whipple shield is the protective layer of armour that covers the outside of a spacecraft. For the past few decades, engineers have been conducting tests to determine just what kind of Whipple shield works best.

To test the strength of Whipple shield materials, researchers simulate conditions in space. They set up a type of firing range using these materials as targets. Instead of blasting actual space debris at the shields, they use aluminum pellets ranging in size from tiny peas to hefty marbles. To set the pellets in high-speed motion, they fire them from super-charged rifles. After each test, researchers examine the damage, then use computer simulations to predict the damage that might be done in space.

What scientists have learned from these tests has helped them improve the design of Whipple shields. They've found that several layers of thin material work better than a single thick layer. In one test, a pea-sized pellet blasted a hole 2 centimetres wide out of a chunk of metal the thickness of your finger. When an identical size pellet was fired at thinner, multiple layers of the same material, the damage was far less. The pellet penetrated the outer layers, but shattered when it bounced off the inner layers.

◆ ◆ ◆

Garbage can be dangerous right here on earth too.

When a tornado or hurricane whips through town, no one is safe. These storm systems can flatten even the sturdiest of homes. But often it's not the high winds alone that deal death and destruction. It's also the debris they unleash, debris than can hit anything left standing.

Winds inside tornadoes can reach speeds of 400 kilometres per hour while hurricanes often reach 210 kilometres per hour. When winds like these uproot trees, shred shingles and rip boards off buildings, they hurl them through the air like missiles. Flying debris can punch holes in walls and smash windows, giving the high-pressure wind an opening so it can wreck houses from the inside. A punctured home is a weakened one.

Engineers and architects who build storm-proof homes need to find out how much stress their materials will handle, and if they will withstand the forces of nature. One test uses a lethal-looking device called a lumber cannon. It has a long barrel of plastic piping, powered by an air compressor. To use it, engineers load long two-by-four boards in one end, turn on the compressor, aim and fire. The boards whip out at hurricane speed, shoot across the laboratory, and pound the test material with deadly blows. Materials and designs that survive the impact may eventually be used to construct sturdier homes in storm-prone areas.

Fly Like a Bird

Before the Wright brothers took to the air, there was Otto Lilienthal, the original birdman.

More than anything else, Lilienthal wanted to fly, so almost every day from 1891 to 1896 he did what no other human dared. He strapped a leather harness to his back, attached a pair of bird-like wings to his arms, ran down a steep hill and threw himself over the edge.

Lilienthal's passion for flying started when he was a young boy living in Germany. He observed birds in flight and dreamed of the day he could fly like one. With his brother's help, he built and tested model gliders that had bird-like wings. When he got older he constructed giant gliders and tried flying these himself.

Lilienthal made full-sized wings by fastening waxed cotton cloth to a frame made out of lightweight bamboo and willow branches. To the wings, he attached a leather harness. By pushing his arms through the harness, he was able to strap the wings to his back. That left his legs and body free to balance and control the glider.

Lilienthal used his glider for the first time in 1891. To achieve liftoff he ran for a short distance while keeping the wings outstretched, then bounced on a springboard he had constructed.

He had enough speed and height for air currents to sweep over the wings, buoying him up for a few seconds.

The experiment was a success, but for Lilienthal it was not enough. He wanted to swoop and soar like a bird, not just bounce into the air. He took his glider to a gravel pit near his home and tried leaping off a hill. This time he flew almost a hundred metres, something no human had done before. Greatly encouraged, he constructed an artificial hill so that he could launch himself into the wind in any direction. Between 1891 and 1896, Lilienthal built dozens of different gliders, each one an improvement on the other. And almost every day during those five years, he would strap on a pair of wings, run down the hill and soar like a bird. So regular and predictable were his takeoffs that photographers from around the world lined up to shoot pictures of him. Lilienthal became famous and his efforts inspired other daredevils to try flying too.

All of that ended on August 9, 1896. That day a sudden gust of wind stalled Lilienthal's glider. It plunged to the ground, killing him. Ironically, Lilienthal had actually designed but not yet built a glider with a controllable rear section — one that could possibly have saved him from the very disaster which ended his life.

More EXtremes

• **Wilbur and Orville Wright took Lilienthal's work one giant step further. From their bicycle shop in Dayton, Ohio, they built a lightweight engine and fastened it to a glider. They added a wooden propeller and equipped the glider with rudders, wing flaps and a pulley system that allowed them to twist the wings in mid-flight. With these controls, they could manoeuvre their aircraft — which they nicknamed the *Flyer* — in**

ways never possible before.

On December 14, 1903, Wilbur climbed aboard and lay flat in the middle of the plane. The engine roared; the *Flyer* bumped down the takeoff track, reared upward for a moment, then lost its lift and crashed into the sand. Wilbur was unhurt; the plane only slightly damaged.

Three days later the Wrights were ready to try again. This time Orville manned the controls as the *Flyer* raced down the track and took to the sky. This flight lasted 12 seconds, covered a distance of over 36 metres and made aviation history as the first ever powered flight.

• American aeronautics engineer Paul MacCready added new meaning to the expression "flying like a bird." In 1977 he used balsa wood, cardboard, Mylar plastic and wire to construct a lightweight flying machine called the *Gossamer Condor*. Its single propeller was powered by a cyclist pedalling a bicycle-like device, and it was steered by twisting the wing tips. The *Gossamer Condor* was the world's first successful human-powered flying machine.

Danger in Mid-Air

Observers in San Diego, California who peered into the sky on August 27, 1923, might have seen two biplanes flying over the city. Not an unusual sight — unless they also saw the long hose connecting the two planes, and realized that at that moment 200 litres of explosive gasoline was being passed from one plane to the other.

In the early days of airplanes, distances were a problem. Small planes carried limited amounts of fuel and could only go short distances at a time. Aircraft designers looked for ways to make planes travel farther without the nuisance of having to land to refuel. One solution — a method still used today — was brilliant, but dangerous: refuel in mid-air. Pass fuel from one plane to another while both planes are in flight.

Lowell Smith piloted the biplane that made the first mid-air refuelling attempt over San Diego. Paul Richter sat in the open rear cockpit. Above their plane flew another. To the untrained eye, it looked no different than most planes, but it was equipped with extra fuel tanks and an unusually long (15-metre) hose. As the pilot of the upper plane edged ahead of the lower one, another man sat in its rear cockpit doling out the hose, aiming it directly at Richter's outstretched hands.

The plan was simple, but extremely risky. Once Richter had a firm grip on the hose, he would open its release valve so fuel could flow from the upper plane into his own plane's tanks. Then the men would fly into the pages of history, becoming the first to make a successful in-flight refuelling.

On the first attempt Richter perched precariously in the open cockpit immediately behind Smith. As he grabbed the dangling hose his fingers accidentally knocked open the release valve, dumping fuel all over himself and the plane. He was only an arm's length away from the hot engine — a single spark would have sent him and the plane up in flames. Fortunately, the slipstream from the spinning propeller whipped the fuel to the back of the plane.

With both pilots struggling to match each other's speed and to keep the distance between the planes constant, Richter jammed the nozzle into his nearly empty fuel tank and opened the valve. In a matter of minutes, 200 litres of gasoline flowed down the hose and into the tanks. The world's first in-flight refuelling attempt was a success.

But the flight wasn't over. To prove the usefulness of in-flight refuelling, Smith and Richter flew on, emptying their tanks again and again. Each time their fuel levels dropped, the second plane pulled ahead, the hose was dropped and another transfer was made. Fighting exhaustion, Smith and Richter flew for 37 hours and 15 minutes, making a total of sixteen successful transfers and establishing a new record for continuous flight.

More EXtremes

- In 1986 Jeana Yeager and Dick Rutan achieved a record for continuous flight of their own. Using an experimental aircraft called *Voyager*, the two flew around the world without once touching down to refuel.

  Voyager had been designed with special features to do the job. It had two engines, one for takeoff and a smaller one for cruising through the air. It was constructed of lightweight materials to economize on fuel. But *Voyager*'s most unusual feature was its wings. It had an H-shape design, with a large main wing near the rear of the plane, a smaller stabilizing wing near the front, and booms on either side of the plane connecting the two. The wings and boom were loaded with highly flammable fuel — 4500 litres of it.

  Space aboard the plane was limited. The quarters were cramped and only one person at a time could sit at the controls. The other had to stretch out flat in the space behind. Rutan and Yeager alternated positions, resting fitfully for two or three hours at a time or gulping down one of the pre-cooked meals they had brought with them.

**Most of their time, however, was
spent keeping the plane in balance.
The fuel was held in seventeen
separate tanks, and as it burned its
weight shifted. To keep the plane
balanced, fuel had to be redistributed
by pumping it from one tank to
another.**

**Rutan and Yeager left Edwards Air
Force Base in California on December
14, 1986. They returned nine days
later after circling the globe — a day
ahead of schedule, but not a moment
too soon. *Voyager* had only 68 litres of
fuel left in its tanks.**

Iced to Death

Most pilots avoid cold fronts, plunging temperatures and dark storm
clouds. Not Russell Colley and Wesley Smith. That's what they
hoped to find.

Colley was a young engineer who was trying to solve a
dangerous problem encountered by airplanes in the early days of
aviation — ice. At high altitudes, moisture froze on the wings of the
plane, forming layers of ice. The ice changed the shape of the wing,
causing air flowing over it to push the plane down rather than lift it
up. The loss of lift forced planes to the ground, often with disastrous
results.

Colley invented a pneumatic de-icing system to solve the
problem. Long rubber strips containing inflatable tubes were

installed on the leading edge of the plane's wing. The tubes could be inflated and deflated, allowing the wing to change shape. The resulting pulsing action cracked the ice, causing it to fall off and be blown away by the plane's slipstream.

The design worked well in wind tunnel tests on the ground. But would it work under actual flight conditions? There was only one way to find out. Take the plane to the sky, find a pocket of freezing rain, and fly into it.

With Smith at the controls and Colley sitting in the forward compartment of a biplane, the two flew over Cleveland, Ohio. They climbed high and before long found a freezing zone. As they hoped, moisture settled on the wings, forming a layer of ice. Colley operated a bicycle hand pump and inflated the tubes along one wing. The tubes bulged, cracking the ice. Air movement did the rest. The ice flaked and crumbled, slithering off the wing like butter off a hot knife. Then Colley switched a two-way valve on the pump, directed air into tubes along the other wing, and did the same to it.

But the plane picked up ice faster than expected. The ice broke away in heavy, uneven chunks. The wings began to sag and vibrate dangerously. The plane's engine growled in protest under the extra weight. Pumping furiously, first one wing then the other, Colley struggled to keep up.

Despite the nail-biting excitement, Smith landed the plane safely and the experiment was declared a success. Colley's de-icing system was installed on other planes, saving many lives and making flights into freezing conditions safer and more routine.

Extreme Facts

- **A layer as thin as a dime on an upper wing surface can increase drag and reduce airplane lift by 25 percent.**

- **Pilots are often daredevils. In 1943 U.S. Colonel Joseph P. Duckworth became the first pilot to fly intentionally into the eye of a hurricane. Since then other hurricane hunters have repeated the daredevil act, often flying directly into storms with winds of 210 kilometres per hour or higher. The data obtained from such flights allows forecasters to track hurricanes and predict their movements accurately.**

3 . . . 2 . . . 1 . . . Blastoff!

Rockets, manned flight, the Apollo and space shuttle missions — these might never have taken place had it not been for a man named Robert Goddard.

Goddard was obsessed with space travel. At a time when most people were trading in their horses for automobiles, and airplanes hadn't yet been invented, Goddard was already planning to put a man on the moon.

But how? Goddard filled notebooks with sketches for all kinds of launchers, everything from giant catapults to monstrous cannons. None of these seemed right for the job. In the end, it was his childhood interest in explosives that gave him the idea to build a rocket.

As a boy he had stuffed the black powder from fireworks into hollow tubes, attached fuses and set them ablaze. More often than not the tubes exploded into bits, but sometimes they shot up a short distance before disintegrating.

Goddard became convinced that he was on to something revolutionary. A rocket of just the right size and shape, with just the right blend of fuel, might be able to travel fast enough and high enough to escape the pull of earth's gravity.

He began the delicate task of designing his machine. Gunpowder and dynamite were quick to burn and simple to use, but they didn't pack enough punch to lift a rocket. Liquid fuels were more powerful, but also more complicated and dangerous.

For almost twenty years, Goddard carried out his own research, often in secrecy to avoid ridicule from others who considered his ideas bizarre. He built rocket after rocket, hauling each one out to a remote field to launch it. Some exploded on the spot. Others fizzled and failed. Occasionally one would lift off the ground, rise a little, then come crashing down.

On a cold day in March, 1926, Goddard loaded his latest design, a 5-metre missile he called *Nell*, into an open car and toted it to his Aunt Effie's nearby farm. He set it up in a snowy field and started a ten-second countdown while an assistant ignited the rocket with a blowtorch strapped onto the end of long pole. For a moment the rocket did nothing. Then it sputtered to life, leaped from the ground, and roared across the field before crashing into a frozen cabbage patch. The whole flight lasted just two and a half seconds, but it was remarkable.

In following years Goddard built larger and more powerful versions of *Nell*. He added fins for stability, gyroscopes for steering, and multi-firing stages for extra boosts of speed. As his rockets grew in size, so did their capabilities. He built rockets that flew faster than the speed of sound, and soared several kilometres into the atmosphere.

By the time he died in 1945, Goddard's risk-taking had been worth it. Even his harshest critics had to admit that the dream of putting a man into space was not so far-fetched after all.

More Extremes

- **Gerald Bull, a Canadian ballistics expert, took one of Goddard's ideas a step further. While testing missiles for the government in the 1960s, Bull had a wild brain wave. If weapons could be fired into space, why not satellites and other scientific instruments?**

  He set about designing an oversized cannon so powerful that it could launch objects directly into space without the use of expensive rockets. He moved to Barbados, redesigned an old naval gun to suit his needs, and began a series of high-altitude tests. With this primitive cannon he found he could launch a projectile 180 kilometres into the atmosphere — not high enough or fast enough to achieve orbit, but promising nevertheless.

  Then things turned sour. To raise money for his project, Bull began dealing with military agencies around the world that were anxious to improve the launching capabilities of their weapons. After being contracted by the Iraqi government to build a cannon that could strike Israel, Gerald Bull was assassinated. His assassin has never been found.

The Ultimate Test

Yuri Gagarin had plenty of time to ponder his fate. Strapped in a tiny one-man capsule perched high above the Soviet rocket that was to hurl him skywards, Gagarin — the world's first full-fledged astronaut — had ninety minutes to wait before blastoff.

Gagarin thought about earlier test flights. They had all been unmanned. One rocket had been lost in space; another blew up in mid-air. Recent ones had been more successful. Gagarin forced himself to think about these. Just months earlier, two dogs had been sent into space, then returned to earth.

Gagarin thought about other dangers he was about to face and about the questions no one had been able to answer. Would he be able to survive without gravity? he wondered. Would his blood still flow freely? Would he choke on his food? Worse still, would his mind be altered, leaving him disoriented and unable to think clearly?

The minutes ticked by. Gagarin's eyes were drawn to the lights, buttons and switches of the control panel. Control panel? How ironic. For Gagarin knew that soon he would have almost no control over the matters that were about to take place. If all went well his hands would hardly touch the instruments. The flight would be directed from the ground. If there was a malfunction, though, some emergency, then it would be different. In that case he had an envelope to open, one that contained a code that would allow him to operate the controls manually.

At 9:05 a.m., April 12, 1961, the engines ignited and the *Vostok* rocket rumbled and shook. "*Poyekhali!*," (We're off!) Gagarin said. With flames and smoke belching from its engines, the rocket struggled off the launch pad, lifting slowly at first, then gaining speed as it rose higher. Within minutes the two-stage rocket separated, propelling the capsule into space.

Nine minutes after blastoff, Gagarin was orbiting above the planet, the first human to ever do so.

His trip lasted 108 minutes. During the flight he made one

revolution around the earth. He radioed greetings from the Soviet people and ate and drank to test for the effects of weightlessness. At 10:25 a.m., as he passed over West Africa, retro rockets fired, slowing the capsule and sending it back into the earth's atmosphere.

At an altitude of 8000 metres a hatch on the capsule blew off, firing Gagarin and his ejector seat into the air. A parachute unfolded and the world's first astronaut floated to earth, landing in a potato field. At first, his bright orange spacesuit and white helmet frightened the woman and her daughter who spotted him. "Are you from outer space?" one timidly asked. Then other farm workers arrived. They had been listening to the radio. "It's Yuri Gagarin! It's Yuri Gagarin!" one shouted. Like long-lost relatives, the workers hugged and kissed him.

"I must report my return to earth," he managed to say at last.

Gagarin was heralded as a hero by the Soviet people. He was awarded a medal and named commander of the Soviet space team.

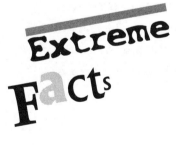

Extreme Facts

- **Unknown to Gagarin at the time, the re-entry did not go as planned. His capsule was supposed to separate from an equipment module, but both craft entered the earth's atmosphere still attached. Fortunately, the heat of re-entry burned the electrical cables holding the two together, allowing them to separate at the last minute.**
- **Besides being the first human in space, Gagarin claimed another first. He was the first person to actually see the earth's round shape, something impossible for a person to do except from space.**

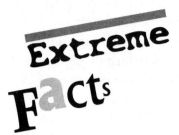

- Gagarin died in the heroic manner that he lived. On March 27, 1968, he was killed on a training flight in a two-seat MIG IJ jet.

- Space flight can still be extremely dangerous. In 1986 the whole world watched as the space shuttle *Challenger*, on a mission to conduct experiments in fluid dynamics as well as to deploy satellites that would track Halley's comet, launched into space. *Challenger* carried six crew plus school teacher Christa McAuliffe. But what looked like the trip of a lifetime ended when the shuttle exploded just after takeoff, killing all the people aboard it. However, there are other brave people to take the place of adventurers like McAuliffe. Barbara Morgan, another teacher who trained at NASA with McAuliffe, expects to be in space as early as the year 2000, as part of NASA's Teacher-in-Space program.

Apollo 11

Eight short years after Gagarin's epic flight, three American astronauts took space travel a giant step forward by travelling to the moon and landing on it. Like Gagarin, their lives depended upon newly developed technology that had never been tested in space.

Neil Armstrong, Edwin (Buzz) Aldrin and Michael Collins were aboard *Apollo 11* on its mission to put a man on the moon. Attached to *Columbia*, their command capsule, was a spindly, spider-like lunar module that had been nicknamed the *Eagle*. According to NASA's plans, once *Columbia* was safely in lunar orbit, the *Eagle* would carry Armstrong and Aldrin to the surface of the moon and then back again.

NASA engineers had spent many years designing the *Eagle*. They were confident of its safety and reliability. The ultimate test, however, was not in controlled laboratories on earth. It would be in unpredictable conditions on the moon. Would the *Eagle* detach itself as planned from *Columbia* once it was in lunar orbit? After carrying its human cargo down to the moon, would it have enough fuel to return? Would all the instruments function as required? No one knew for certain.

The first part of the lunar mission was the most hair-raising. During its descent, one of *Eagle's* computers malfunctioned. The lunar module began to drift off course and headed for a crater strewn with boulders the size of cars. Armstrong switched to manual override, put the module under his own control, then steered it for a clearing beyond the boulders. The module thumped to a landing with seconds of fuel in its descent stage remaining.

The rest of the mission went as planned. After spending several hours on the moon's surface collecting rocks, setting up experiments and taking photographs, Armstrong and Aldrin fired *Eagle's* ascent engines, docked with *Columbia*, and made a triumphant journey back to earth.

More EXtremes

• *Apollo 13*, on its way to making the third manned moon landing, showed just how nerve-wracking space travel can be. Astronauts Jim Lovell, Fred Haise and Jack Swigert were approaching the moon in 1970 when they heard a loud bang and felt the spacecraft shudder. One oxygen tank had exploded and another had dumped its oxygen into space. With their life-support systems rapidly failing, the crew moved into the much smaller lunar module. Quickly they made drastic changes to their plans. Instead of continuing to the moon and landing there, they fired the lunar module's engines to alter its course and return to earth.

Over the next four days, the astronauts' equipment malfunctioned, cabin temperatures plunged and levels of lethal carbon dioxide climbed, as the men's supplies of water and oxygen dwindled. NASA hoped for the best, but prepared for the worst. President Nixon prepared a memorial to deliver to the nation in the event that NASA could not bring the astronauts safely home.

As the spacecraft neared earth the crew left the lunar module and returned to the crippled command

**module. Minutes before re-entry, the
lunar module was uncoupled.
Strapped to their seats, the crew
braved a blazing ride through earth's
atmosphere, not knowing until the
last minute if there would be enough
power left to operate the parachutes
that would slow their descent.
Fortunately, all ended well. *Apollo 13*
landed safely in the ocean, a short
distance from its rescue ship.**

Dateline: Science
International Space Station Scientists

On one shuttle mission, astronauts carried two spiders, Arabella
and Anita. They also took 2 minnows, 50 minnow eggs, 6 mice and
720 fruit flies.

At first Arabella and Anita were confused and wove sloppy,
crooked webs. The minnows had problems too. They swam in
circles. But then, as the flight continued, things returned to normal.
The spiders' webs became neater and more even. The minnows
stopped their crazed swimming.

These creatures were part of carefully planned experiments to
study the effects of weightlessness.

On earth, gravity often interferes with experiments. It forces air
to rise or drop, liquids to separate, crystals to grow in irregular ways,
roots of plants to dive down and stems to shoot up. In space, where
there is no "up" or "down," scientists can do experiments without
disruption from gravity.

In the past few decades, hundreds of zero-gravity experiments
were carried out in Spacelab, a reusable laboratory mounted inside
the cargo bay of NASA's Space Shuttle. From the year 2004 onwards,

these experiments will be conducted in the International Space Station, a massive space laboratory four times larger than the Russian Mir space station.

The International Space Station (ISS) is a joint undertaking of sixteen nations. Each participating country is adding its own special elements and expertise to the final assembly of the station. Canada is providing the 17-metre robotic arm. The United States is providing three connecting modules. Russia is adding two more — though Russia's attempts to keep the Mir space station running have significantly affected they work they planned to have completed on the ISS. Brazil and Italy are contributing specialized equipment.

Components for the International Space Station are being launched into space, where they will be assembled by astronauts. In all, it will take forty-five separate missions and over 850 hours of dangerous space walks to complete the job of piecing together the largest and most complicated space project ever undertaken.

Then the real fun begins. That's when mission specialists — astronauts who are also scientists and engineers — will begin their work. Hundreds of research projects are being planned, everything from investigating how zero-gravity conditions affect bones and tissues, to finding out how to make better metal alloys.

In the end, the whole world will benefit as mission specialists unravel mysteries and make discoveries in chemistry, medicine, space and technology.

Rocket Man

Harold Graham had twenty seconds to prove the worth of the bulky contraption on his back. Twenty seconds to blast skywards, scoot a short distance, and land safely . . . or die trying.

Strapped to Graham's back was a wild and dangerous device. In some ways it resembled the scuba gear carried by divers. It had two tanks and a system of hoses and nozzles. But instead of guiding Graham below the ocean surface, this device fired him aloft.

The contraption was called a rocket belt. It had been invented by Wendell Moore, an engineer who worked for Bell Aerosystems in the 1950s. Mostly made from spare parts, the rocket belt had two tanks filled with hydrogen peroxide. The fuel was fed over a fine metal screen which changed it to steam. When the steam was forced through a pair of nozzles, it unleashed enough thrust to shoot a person upward.

Graham, a young engineering student, volunteered to test the device. On April 20, 1961, near the airport in Niagara Falls, New York, he strapped the heavy equipment to his back. In each hand he held throttles similar to those used to play video games. By pressing on the throttles, he could control the force and direction of the steam coming from the nozzles. Graham had just enough fuel in his tanks for a twenty-second flight. If he flew too high or went too far and ran short of fuel, he would crash to the ground. Timing was everything.

When he was ready, Graham engaged the rockets. A blast of steam erupted from the tanks with an ear-shattering screech. Graham slowly rose up out of the cloud of steam. High above the ground he adjusted the throttles and zipped ahead a short distance, hovered for a moment, then gracefully lowered himself to the ground.

As brief as it was, Graham's flight made rocket history and proved that free-wheeling human flight was entirely possible.

- The rocket belt was originally developed so that soldiers could fly, hover and drop into combat with pin-point accuracy.
- Newer versions of the rocket belt have been used in some famous demonstrations. In the James Bond movie *Thunderball*, stuntman Bill Suitor (substituting for actor Sean Connery) donned a rocket belt and flew over buildings. In 1984 Suitor rocketed into a Los Angeles stadium for the opening ceremonies of the Olympic Games.
- Millennium Jet, Inc., an aerospace company, is developing and testing a modern day version of the rocket man gear. The SoloTrek Exo-Skeletor Flying Vehicle (XFV) looks a bit like an open-frame, twin-blade helicopter for one person. The operator steps onto the machine, snaps on a safety harness and powers up a gasoline-operated engine that churns the blades and brings the device to life. With the SoloTrek XFV, the operator can take off vertically, dash horizontally at speeds up to 130 kilometres per hour, and land on demand on a surface not much bigger than a dining room table.

Walk on the Wild Side

Edward White was 200 kilometres above the Pacific Ocean when he stepped outside for a walk. The view was spectacular, the dangers very real.

White was an astronaut aboard *Gemini 4*, a 1965 NASA space mission. *Gemini 4* was to orbit the earth, then return its human cargo to a safe landing in the Atlantic Ocean. Pretty tame as far as space journeys were concerned . . . with one big difference. Early in the mission, White was to leave the safety of his capsule for a walk outside, wearing a suit and carrying gear that had been tested on earth, but never in space.

White's suit had special features. A long gold-plated "umbilical" cord connected the suit to the spacecraft and fed him a steady stream of oxygen and electricity. Strapped to White's chest was an oxygen pack, a back-up supply in case the cord became severed or the system failed. To shield his eyes from the brilliant glare of the sun, White wore a helmet with a tinted visor. The suit itself was composed of multiple layers of material, protection from the extreme temperatures of space: 120°C in direct sunlight, −65°C in the shade. The extra layers also protected White from other hazards. They screened deadly cosmic radiation and resisted punctures by dust-sized meteorites that wheeled through space faster than bullets from a gun. To manoeuvre himself, White carried a "space pistol," a jet-nozzled propulsion gun.

On June 3, just after *Gemini 4's* third revolution in orbit, White and fellow astronaut James McDivitt depressurized the capsule and opened the hatch. Mission Control held its breath. This was a moment of extreme danger. There was no bulkhead protecting the men, no air-lock separating the capsule from the voids of space. Both men were exposed to the same hazards. Any trouble at this point likely meant death for the two.

White stepped outside and fired the gun to propel himself away from the capsule. Mission Control relaxed slightly. One danger down; several more to go. White coasted for a spell, then fired the gun to change directions, then again to tumble forward. The gun worked as planned. Would the protective suit hold up as well? One small puncture, one tiny tear would spell death. Without his pressurized environment, White's blood would boil in seconds and he would explode like an overinflated balloon.

For twenty-one minutes White manoeuvred through space, testing the gun and growing more confident in his ability to control his movements. Although he was scheduled to stay outside the capsule for only a short time, he had so much fun that Mission Control had difficulty convincing him to come back inside. Finally his propulsion gun ran out of fuel. Left with no choice, White tugged on his line and worked his way back to the capsule.

The gun and pressurized suit worked as planned, and marked the beginning of a new era in space travel. Today astronauts regularly venture outside of their capsules to do repairs and conduct experiments, but they owe a large debt of gratitude to Edward White, the first American to take the risk.

Buried Alive!

Most victims of avalanches die of suffocation in a matter of minutes. Tom Crowley hoped to beat the odds.

Crowley, an American medical professor who lived in Denver, Colorado, often hiked into the surrounding mountains. He was disturbed by the growing number of avalanche deaths. Crowley knew that most avalanche victims died because of suffocation, and that the chances of survival dropped with each passing minute. Could there be some way of breathing while buried under snow? he wondered.

Crowley mulled over the problem, then one night in 1991 while he lay in bed struggling to fall asleep, an idea popped into his head. Snow, he realized in a flash, was full of air! A minute later he had a plan for a new invention, the AvaLung.

The AvaLung is a lightweight vest designed to be worn by skiers, snowmobilers and hikers who venture into wilderness areas where avalanches are a threat. It has a built-in filtration system. Air from the snow is drawn into the front of the vest and passed along tubing to the victim's mouth through a mouthpiece in the collar. Exhaled carbon dioxide is released through the back of the vest.

Crowley had the first version of the AvaLung ready in 1993. The device passed all laboratory tests, but would it really work under avalanche conditions? To find out, Crowley followed a carefully considered plan. He strapped on the vest and then crawled into a deep pit. Others shovelled almost 2 metres of snow on top of him and packed it down hard. Using a small microphone inside the mouthpiece, Crowley grunted a few times each minute so that those outside would know that he was alive and alert. For over half an hour he stayed in the pit, surrounded by blackness and cold, drawing in air through the mouthpiece.

Since that first successful test, the AvaLung has undergone many more. Each "burial" has been conducted under strict conditions to ensure safety for those involved. The buried tester wears a radio communication device to allow contact with surface workers at all times. Emergency medical services are available at the site, and sensors attached to the tester's body measure oxygen and carbon dioxide levels.

Dateline: Science
Forging a Sneak Attack

When an avalanche strikes, huge amounts of snow — some in slabs as big as refrigerators and as hard as rocks — thunder down a slope at incredible speeds, sweeping away anything in the way.

Forecasting and controlling avalanches is important stuff. To do the job properly, an avalanche scientist needs to understand the nature of snow and the conditions that change it.

Snow settles into layers known as the snowpack. Older harder snow lies underneath fresher softer snow. What cements one layer to another are the tiny crystals that make up snow itself. Normally these are pointy, almost star-shaped. If wind and weather conditions are just so, the points break off. These crystals pack together snugly and lock into one another. Square- or triangular-shaped crystals, however, don't bond as readily. They form weaker layers that are likely to slip away at a moment's notice.

To determine the stability of the snowpack, avalanche scientists often head into dangerous areas — those with a high possibility of avalanche — to obtain samples.

One of the simplest and safest tests is the hand test. By pushing objects into the snow pack, a scientist can judge the hardness of layers. Crusty layers over soft layers scream danger.

When an avalanche looks likely, the avalanche specialist brings out weapons to combat it. Using everything from hand-tossed charges to the "Avalauncher," a specialized cannon that uses compressed nitrogen to fire explosives, they blast the unstable area. By bringing the snow down in a systematic and safe way, avalanche forecasters hope to surprise the enemy before it sneaks an attack of its own.

Extreme Facts

- Most avalanches occur during snowstorms.
- 90 percent of all avalanches involving humans are triggered by their victims.
- There are two types of avalanches: loose snow and slab avalanches. Loose snow avalanches are less dangerous. They begin from a single point and fan outwards like an upside-down V as they come down the mountain. Slab avalanches are a greater threat. When one layer of snow has not bonded well to others, it can break off in huge slabs and crash down the mountain with terrific force and speed.
- A number system from 1 to 5 is used to classify avalanches based on their size and the amount of material they contain. A class 1 avalanche could knock people over, but not completely bury them. A class 5, on the other hand, could destroy a whole town or forest.
- Canada's worst snow disaster occurred in 1910 when an avalanche ripped down a mountain at Roger's Pass, British Columbia, killing sixty-two workmen who were trying to remove snow from an earlier avalanche.

High-Altitude Surfers

For Bertrand Piccard and Brian Jones, it was like surfing. They'd catch a high-speed wave, sway and roll with it, then ride it until it died. Only the men weren't in the water. They were high above the clouds, cruising on a jet stream at 250 kilometres per hour. And instead of a surfboard, they were riding a high-tech balloon.

Piccard and Jones were attempting to do something twenty earlier daredevil teams had failed to accomplish — become the first balloonists to fly around the world non-stop. It was no small feat. Dozens of other adventurers had tried the same thing. All had failed. Some had plunged out of the sky into the ocean, others stalled in remote mountains or, if they were lucky, simply cascaded to earth in a billow of fabric and broken dreams.

The dangers of such a flight were all too real. Balloons don't have engines or propellers to push them along. They don't have rudders or other steering devices either. At the mercy of winds, all balloonists can do is change altitude, dodge storm systems and rise or fall to catch high-speed jet streams.

Jet streams blow at altitudes of 7000 to 12 000 metres. At these heights, the air is thin, oxygen levels are low, and temperatures often drop to −56°C. To survive a journey around the world at these altitudes, balloonists need a pressurized and heated cabin. Any mechanical breakdown, any instrument failure — no matter how slight — would put their lives in peril.

Piccard and Jones had technology on their side, however. And money. Lots of it. Their cone-shaped balloon, *Breitling Orbiter 3* — a towering hulk of silver fabric — cost $3 million to produce. It had features earlier balloons lacked, and was equipped with the latest in high-tech instruments.

Breitling Orbiter 3 was actually several balloons in one. An inner helium-filled cell provided most of the lift for the balloon. Wrapped around this was another balloon layer, a jacket of hot air that heated the helium gas, giving it even greater lift. Topping the whole thing, and giving *Orbiter 3* a distinctive cone shape, was yet another smaller helium balloon. All told, *Orbiter 3* contained enough gas to fill seven Olympic-sized swimming pools.

Instead of using kerosene to heat the air in the balloon, as earlier versions had, *Orbiter 3* used propane, a heavier but more reliable fuel. A pressurized gondola below the balloon was equipped with a kitchen, bunk, toilet and high-tech communications devices such as a fax machine and satellite phone. Batteries and solar panels supplied power for the onboard equipment.

With all of these innovations to the balloon, Piccard and Jones were ready for the ultimate test — to travel around the world without stopping. They started their journey with a liftoff from the mountains of Switzerland on March 1, 1999. The balloonists drifted southward and then eastward across Europe, toward Africa, changing altitude as they searched for jet streams to carry them further east. They were lucky. On the fourth day they moved into a jet stream travelling at 95 kilometres per hour. It blew them towards India. After that, it was like playing tag, slipping from one jet stream to catch another, surfing the wild winds, and riding them as far east as they could go.

There were a few snags along the way. Over Mexico, the balloon popped out of its jet stream and started heading the wrong way. Another time, a heater failed and temperatures dropped to 8°C. But luck prevailed. As the balloon swung over the Atlantic it caught a 160 kilometre per hour wind that all but blew it home.

On March 20, nineteen days after starting off, *Breitling Orbiter 3* landed in the Egyptian desert after winding its way around the world, a distance of almost 43 000 kilometres. Piccard and Jones had set a world record, and proved that with the help of technology, the impossible could become possible.

3

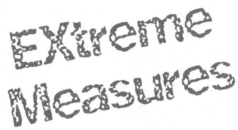

EXtreme Measures

Breaking barriers . . . conquering the unknown

Every great **achievement** was once
considered impossible.

Evan Rosenberg

While many people are grabbing briefcases, hopping into cars and driving to work, oceanographer Karen Van Damm is cramming herself into a tiny submersible and heading to the ocean floor. Plunging into the ocean to collect information is as routine to her as going to the office is to others. Only it's riskier at times . . .

Take her 1991 trip to the bottom of the Pacific Ocean. Van Damm and other scientists aboard the submersible *Alvin* were revisiting a site in the Pacific Ocean they had explored only fifteen months earlier. On the first visit, the ocean floor had been teeming with tiny crabs, small fish and exotic tube worms. This time the area resembled a war zone. Jets of scorching water blasted from cracks in the rocky bottom, shooting plumes of white material 45 metres above the sea floor. The sea bed was covered in ash. Beneath the blanket of grey, the scientists discovered thousands of chunks of dead flesh — the scorched and shredded remains of life. A sudden explosive event, perhaps only hours earlier, had devastated the area, cutting the animals to pieces, burning their bodies and raining ash upon them.

The crew aboard *Alvin* witnessed something no one had ever seen before — the after-effects of a violent eruption on the ocean floor. Just before their visit, molten magma from deep inside the earth had blasted through fissures in the rock, carrying with it streams of superheated water and clouds of bacteria. When the magma hit the cold sea floor, it hardened in an instant and splintered into shards of glass. The rushing water, flying glass and extreme temperatures dealt a fatal blow to life in the area, tearing up bodies and frying flesh in an instant. Had the *Alvin's* crew been at the site at the time of the eruption . . . "After coming this close," Van Damm said, "I don't want to see red lava flowing on the sea floor. A few days later is close enough for me."

In their quest to gather information, scientists sometimes go where others dare not venture. They take risks, brave discomforts, and dedicate their time to collecting data and evidence. In the pursuit of truth, they take extreme measures.

Body Snatcher

Andreas Vesalius was willing to go to almost any lengths to prove his point . . . even if it meant snatching corpses and smuggling them home.

As a boy living in France in the early 1500s, Andreas Vesalius collected bones the way some people collect coins. He dissected animals, large and small, drew detailed pictures of the bones, and labelled each one. For an extra challenge he sometimes reassembled the skeletons, piecing the bones together like an elaborate jigsaw puzzle.

When he became older, Vesalius entered medical school. He loved anatomy class and was thrilled whenever he could lend a hand in a human dissection. But it wasn't long before he made an important discovery — one that would get him in serious trouble the rest of his life.

Vesalius's professors followed the teachings of Claudius Galen, a scientist and doctor who had lived in Rome thirteen hundred years earlier. Galen had written a book about human anatomy, a book that physicians of the time followed faithfully when they did dissections. Vesalius found that many of Galen's descriptions were inaccurate.

Galen said the breastbone had seven parts. Vesalius found only three. The liver had lobes, Galen wrote. Vesalius could not find any. Galen's book was filled with so many errors that Vesalius came to a shocking conclusion: Galen had never dissected a human body in his entire life. His book was based on falsehoods — and for over a thousand years people had blindly accepted it as truth!

Vesalius started a great project to correct the problem. He began to write his own book of anatomy, one that would be truthful and accurate. But that meant Vesalius needed to dissect more bodies. And that was a big problem.

Human dissections were rare events. The human body was considered sacred, so to dissect the dead, even for medical purposes, required special permission. Vesalius was determined to keep his project a secret, even if it meant bending the rules in his favour.

To get bodies for dissection he raided the gallows, where criminals were executed, for their corpses were often left hanging in disgrace after an execution. Over time the bodies would decompose, leaving the bones exposed. Under the cover of darkness Vesalius crept to the gallows, slipped rotting corpses from the ropes and smuggled them home to his laboratory. There he continued his study. He wrote descriptions of his findings and sketched the organs and bones he found.

Eventually his book was complete. When it was published in 1543 it filled 663 pages and contained over 300 detailed drawings showing every part of the human body. But the book angered many. Followers of Galen claimed that it was Vesalius who was wrong, not

Galen. They plotted against him, calling him a heretic and madman. His enemies spread rumours and opposed his appointment as physician to the emperor. Depressed by the storm of protest, Vesalius threw a large part of his manuscript into the fire.

The worst charge against Vesalius, however, came from the family of a young Spanish nobleman. According to the family, when the young man died Vesalius had asked if he could perform an autopsy, but on opening the body he had found the heart still beating. That made Vesalius a murderer, they claimed.

Although none of the charges was ever proved, they damaged Vesalius's reputation and haunted him for the rest of his life. He died on a journey to Jerusalem, alone and far from loved ones, never realizing the true value of his work.

But Vesalius had unleashed a slow wave of change. Gradually his teachings took hold, erasing the shadow of falsehood that had stood for thirteen hundred years. Now he is recognized as a great physician and the father of modern anatomy.

Danger in the Jungle

Richard Spruce wasn't one to give up. Not when he almost lost all of his possessions to a raging river in the South American wilderness. Not when he became partially paralyzed and had to drag himself through the jungle. Not even when he overheard his own murder being plotted.

Spruce was a botanist who left England in 1849 to spend fifteen years exploring and studying the Amazon river system. Along the way he collected specimens of ferns, mosses and flowering plants. His journey was marked by one hardship after another. But Spruce was a survivor. He handled each difficulty in clever and resourceful ways.

One time he built a rope-and-bamboo bridge to cross a river

that was impossible to navigate. Another time, on a trek up a steep mountain in Ecuador, Spruce passed out from exhaustion . . . and recovered just as condors swooped down from the sky to attack him. Yet another time he overheard strangers in a village plotting to kill him. But he didn't panic. That night he hid in his canoe, his gun at his side. At daybreak he escaped.

Spruce kept careful records of his journey. He mapped his route and kept a journal of his discoveries and observations. But the long expedition took its toll on his health, and Spruce became weaker with each passing year.

Eventually he lost the hearing in one ear and became partially paralyzed in one leg. Still he refused to give up. Using a wooden staff for support, he dragged himself through the jungle.

By 1864, however, Spruce was forced by ill health to return to England. He spent his last years writing scientific reports of his travels through South America. In his lifetime he accomplished what few others could even dream, the scientific exploration of the Amazon river basin.

Dateline: Science
Filling the World's Medicine Chest

Deep in the world's rainforests a handful of scientists scour the forest, carefully examining its plants. They collect samples and seeds. Above all they talk to the native peoples, hoping to learn all that they can before it is too late. For the rainforests are disappearing at an alarming rate . . . and so is the world's medicine chest.

One out of every four medicines we use today is derived from plants. And almost a quarter of those come from the rainforest. As the rainforests disappear, so do many of the plants that cure diseases. This has stirred scientists to action, sending them into the rainforest to find out more while it's still possible.

Scientists can learn much from the people who already live there.

Most tribes have a healer or shaman who has experience in using local plants to cure the sick. By interviewing these experts, scientists can learn more about healing plants from that area.

The work of these scientists is demanding and difficult. The hours are long, the weather hot and muggy, and dangers from animals, insects and disease are real. But there are many rewards. Not long ago, for example, scientists discovered the amazing medicinal benefits of the rosy periwinkle, a plant from the rainforests of Madagascar. It was being used by a shaman as a treatment for diabetes. Scientists found that it contained over eighty chemical compounds. Six of them were proven helpful in fighting cancer. Thanks to the rosy periwinkle, children with leukemia, and people with Hodgkin's disease and other cancers now have an eighty percent chance of long-term survival.

Not to Be Silenced

"There was once a town in the heart of America where all life seemed to live in harmony with its surroundings. . . . Then a strange blight crept over the area and everything began to change . . . "
— Rachel Carson, *Silent Spring*

What is the price of progress? For Rachel Carson, an American marine biologist with a gift for writing, the price people were willing to pay for progress was far too high.

In the 1950s Carson noticed disturbing changes in the environment. Each spring, fewer birds along the American eastern seaboard were returning to their breeding grounds to nest. The eggs they laid — if they laid any at all — were thin-shelled, fragile and likely to shatter at the slightest touch. Some eggs had no shells at all, only a thin membrane covering the quivering yolk. The few hatchlings that did survive were often horribly deformed. And everywhere the sounds of life were fading, replaced instead by an eerie silence.

Carson believed these changes were due to the widespread use of chemical pesticides that farmers across the land sprayed on their crops to rid them of insects and other pests. Those chemical pesticides had side effects, Carson argued. They seeped into the soil and found their way into streams and rivers. Birds and other creatures that fed on insects absorbed the poisons. As the toxic levels inside their bodies climbed, many animals died slow and painful deaths. Others lingered, only to pass the poisons to the next generation.

Today we know much more about the dangers of pesticides and other chemicals, but half a century ago Carson's views were revolutionary — and they did not sit well with government, industry or even farmers. But Carson was passionate about the environment, so in 1962 she published *Silent Spring*, a haunting description of the destruction of wildlife. The book was an instant bestseller. Her words struck nerves and touched hearts across the country.

The chemical industry reacted strongly with a smear campaign to discredit Carson. They threatened lawsuits and called her "a hysterical woman." But the campaign backfired. The protest raised the public's awareness and they sided with Carson. Even President John F. Kennedy was affected by the book. After he read *Silent Spring* he called for the testing of the chemicals mentioned in it. Eventually laws were passed to control the use of pesticides.

Although Rachel Carson died of cancer in 1964, her book sparked a worldwide environmental movement that continues today. Not only environmentalists, but people the world over, owe much to her powerful words.

Hero of the Rainforest

Chico Mendes was a struggling Brazilian tapper — a person who makes a living extracting a type of sap known as latex from rubber trees. In the 1980s he became disturbed by the rapid destruction of the rainforest, usually at the hands of ranchers who wanted to tear down the trees and turn the forest into pasture for grazing cattle.

Mendes encouraged other tappers to join him in a fight to save the rainforest. When an area of forest was targeted for destruction, he would call other tappers to the site. Fifty or sixty tappers would gather, confront the work crews, and try to convince them to stop. Sometimes these encounters turned ugly and violent. Other times they were successful, and a huge section of the rainforest was saved.

In spite of these tactics, the rainforest continued to disappear at an alarming rate. Mendes doubled his efforts. He asked the Brazilian government to step in, buy large areas of the forest, and set them aside as reserves. That way, the land would be protected from ranchers, and tappers could carry out their business in peace. Threatened by the plan, several ranchers plotted to put an end to Chico Mendes and his cause.

On December 22, 1988, as he walked out his back door to take a shower, Mendes was gunned down and killed. His tragic death stirred the government into action. His killers were captured, tried and sentenced to nineteen years in prison. More importantly, stricter laws limiting the destruction of the rainforest were enforced, and huge tracts of land were set aside for conservation. One of the largest of these — an 800 000-hectare region — was named the Chico Mendes Reserve.

More Extremes

Scientists like Rachel Carson — in fact, any radical thinkers who publicize controversial or unpopular views — often have to take a brave stand against a sea of opposition.

- At a time when new ideas were often considered to be works of the devil, Nicolas Copernicus, a sixteenth century astronomer, put his life on the line by publishing his new theory. In the time of Copernicus, most people believed that the sun revolved around the earth. He wrote a book that suggested the exact opposite: the earth and planets revolved around the sun. Today we know this is true, but in the 1500s the idea was revolutionary. Copernicus could have been imprisoned or even executed for voicing his thoughts, but he decided to express them anyway. In the end, he was neither killed nor imprisoned. He died from a stroke on the day his book was published.

- Charles Darwin stewed over his ideas for twenty years before he found the courage to publish them. He feared that once his Theory of Evolution became public, he would be criticized and condemned. He was right. When he finally published *On the Origin of Species* in 1859, he was belittled in

More EXtremes

newspapers and condemned by religious groups who believed his thoughts ran contrary to biblical views of creation. Today Darwin's ideas are widely accepted, and he is honoured for his scientific genius.

• Albert Einstein is a household name today, but when he first voiced his Theory of Relativity in 1905, reaction to it was, "Unbelievable! Impossible!" Einstein had suggested that time and space, matter and energy were linked. Today we know part of that theory as $E = mc^2$ — probably the most famous equation of all time.

But in Einstein's time other scientists found gaps in his thinking and were quick to point them out. In response to these criticisms, Einstein added a new part to his theory in 1915. Large objects with immense gravity cause space-time to bend, he said. That created an even bigger uproar. But in 1919 an experiment conducted during a solar eclipse showed that light rays from distant stars were bent by the gravity of the sun, just as Einstein's theory predicted. Einstein was right, but he had to weather a decade of ridicule before other scientists agreed that his "revolutionary" ideas were, in fact, true.

When winds howl across the plains, when the air thickens with
humidity and black clouds stack up like burnt pancakes in the sky,
conditions are ripe for a storm of tornado proportions.

And while most people run for safety, some scientists hop in
their trucks and drive into the storm's centre. These are tornado
scientists — storm chasers as they are sometimes called. For them,
the approaching storm is a chance to study first-hand one of nature's
most awesome creations.

The United States has the highest average annual number of
tornadoes in the world, about eight hundred a year. Most U.S.
tornadoes develop during spring and summer in an area known as
Tornado Alley. It's a broad swath of land that begins in Texas and
runs northeast like a giant band-aid across the United States. In an
average year hundreds of funnels drop from the sky in Tornado Alley.
Most sputter out in seconds. Others last only five or ten minutes, but
in that time they can churn up massive destruction, even death.

Scientists have been studying the swirling monsters of Tornado
Alley for decades. Most of their work has been from above and
around tornado systems. They've taken temperature, pressure and
humidity readings, recorded shifting wind patterns, used radar to
track storm movements, even taken pictures by satellite. And while
scientists have learned a lot from this kind of work, there are huge
gaps in their understanding of tornadoes. That's why, for some of
them, getting instruments *below* and *inside* tornadoes is so important.

So when storms threaten and tornadoes seem certain, storm
chasers drive to the action, hoping to spot funnels in the making.
Using flatbed trucks and cars with roof racks, they carry an arsenal of
high-tech equipment to take measurements from different locations
around the developing tornado. These include portable Doppler
radar units that help chart rotating wind currents deep inside the
storm system, weather balloons with atmospheric tracking devices,
and videocameras to capture footage of the event. Many storm

chasers carry cell phones, scanners and laptop computers to keep in touch with weather forecasters and each other, so they can find out exactly where the tornado is and how fast it is moving.

Getting a glimpse of the inside of a tornado is the ultimate goal for some storm chasers. Not that they want to get "up close and personal" with a twister to the point of being sucked into its updraft. What they're aiming for is more scientific and a lot more detached — clear video footage from inside the tornado.

Some storm chasers, like Charles Edwards, are close to reaching this goal. Edwards lives in the heart of Tornado Alley, and once built a nearly indestructible videocamera to do the job. Protected with fibreglass layers, weighted down with 48 kilograms of lead ballast, and painted bright orange for easy sighting, his "Dillo-Cam" was dropped in the path of a swirling tornado just moments before it touched down. When the battered camera was later recovered, it featured grainy close-up footage of the tornado — but no clear images of its dark interior. Edwards and his Dillo-Cam are still trying.

To be a storm chaser takes skill and courage, but also patience. Tornadoes are fabulously fickle. Even at the height of tornado season, long days may pass before one makes an appearance. When it does, the tornado may suddenly drop from the sky, wreak havoc, then disappear into thin air once again.

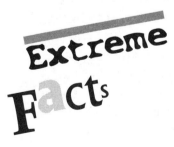

Extreme Facts

- **Tornadoes create the earth's fastest winds — sometimes 500 kilometres per hour or more.**
- **While winds inside a tornado are fast, tornadoes themselves move more slowly across the ground. A tornado can stand still or move forward at speeds up to 110 kilometres per hour.**
- **To measure a tornado's destructive power, storm chasers use a system**

known as the Fujita scale. According to this scale, most tornadoes range from slight (F-0: slight winds, little damage) to severe (F-5: incredible winds, 420-512 kilometres per hour, and houses destroyed or moved).

• The tornado that caused the greatest loss of life along Tornado Alley occurred on March 18, 1925, when a twister called the TriState Tornado tore through Missouri, Illinois and Indiana. For three and a half hours the tornado cut a swath of destruction through a series of mining towns. Almost 700 people were killed and over 2000 injured.

• Scientists hope to learn more about tornadoes through the Tornado Debris Project. Since tornadoes carry debris long distances, recovering traceable items after a storm provides scientists with useful information. Cancelled cheques, photographs with names, bank statements and other items can be traced back to their owners to give scientists information about the starting and ending points of the items' journeys. When combined with data obtained from radar and satellites, they help scientists figure out the tornado's speed, direction and wind patterns.

Dateline: Science
At the Brink of Disaster

In 1991 Maurice Kraft and his wife, Katia, died in a wave of hot gas and ash when Mount Unzen, a volcano in Japan, erupted suddenly. The Krafts were not tourists, out to see a volcano up close. They were volcanologists — volcano scientists — on a mission to study one of the earth's most spectacular and unpredictable phenomena. And their deaths were not unique. In the past fifty years, at least twenty-seven volcano scientists have died in the line of duty.

Many volcanoes occur where the earth's plates collide and push together. Others occur in the middle of plates in areas called hotspots, regions where magma, or molten rock, seeps through the plate and erupts. By studying volcanoes, scientists hope to learn more about the earth's interior and the stresses and strains on its crust.

But there is another reason why their work is important. Over 500 million people live dangerously close to volcanoes. Many dwell in huge cities like Tokyo and Mexico City, where a sudden eruption could spell large-scale disaster. Finding some way of predicting volcanic eruptions so that people could flee to safety has been a dream of volcanologists for many years.

People living near active volcanoes have reported certain signs weeks, even months, before an eruption. The ground shakes, eerie creaks echo from below, and sometimes the earth bulges in spots as molten rock makes its way to the surface. Putrid smells often linger in the air, and animals become mysteriously quiet.

Volcanologists are using these signs as clues in their work. They install seismic equipment in and around the dangerous areas near active volcanoes, hoping to pinpoint even the slightest of tremors. They monitor gases in the area, knowing that an increase in sulphur dioxide may signal an eruption. They also map and measure volcanoes so that any changes in size or shape, no matter how small, can be detected.

Using the data from these studies, volcanologists have improved their forecasting capabilities in recent years. They are often able to detect an eruption hours or sometimes days in advance. Unfortunately, this is still too short a time to give enough advance warning to get people to safety. So the dream continues. In the tradition of brave scientists like Maurice and Katia Kraft, volcanologists continue to trudge up dangerous slopes, to the very edge of bubbling cauldrons, in the hope of improving the odds.

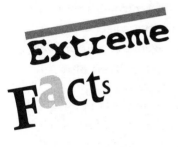

Extreme Facts

- **There are over 1500 active volcanoes on earth, not counting hundreds more under the oceans. In the last 400 years, 583 have erupted.**
- **The major cause of death during an eruption is not lava or rivers of mud. It's clouds of superheated gas and ash that rip down mountains, disintegrating anything in the way.**
- **Volcanic eruptions can be immediate, but their effects can be felt for a long time too. Eruptions spew sulphur-rich gas into the atmosphere. The sulphur mixes with water vapour, forming clouds of sulphuric acid, which can absorb solar radiation and cause climate changes.**
- **In 1992, the year after Mount Pinatubo in the Philippines erupted, temperatures around the world dropped by nearly a full degree.**
- **Lightning strikes can be among the most spectacular side-effects of a volcanic eruption. Friction between**

Extreme Facts

fine particles and gases from the volcano can force huge electrical discharges, putting on a light-and-sound show unlike any other.

• The worst volcanic disaster recorded in world history occurred on August 27, 1883, when the Indonesian island of Krakatoa erupted, killing 30 000 people. The eruption was so violent that it caused tidal waves and sent shock waves to distant parts of the world. The sound of the explosion was heard in Australia, thousands of kilometres away from the site.

A Bold Mission

Two hundred and forty people were on the *HMS Challenger* when it set sail from England in 1872. Far fewer were still aboard when it returned. From the start no one realized how dangerous the voyage would be, how long it would take or how relentless the routine would become.

The *HMS Challenger* was on a bold scientific mission, the first of its kind. Its crew of sailors and scientists travelled the world's vast oceans, mapping, measuring and studying them from top to bottom.

Between 1872 and 1876 *Challenger* circled the globe, crossing one ocean after another. Along the way, the ocean depth was measured, rock and mud were scooped from the bottom, and bottles of sea water were collected. The crew braved hurricanes and tropical storms, bypassed jutting rocks and skirted around crushing ice floes.

Once an enormous wave swept over the ship. Another time the *Challenger* plowed into an iceberg. One sailor was killed when a block and tackle came loose and struck him. Another was accidentally poisoned. Two men drowned. One died of infection. Twenty-six men left the ship as invalids.

For many aboard the ship, however, it was the mind-numbing routine that was hardest to endure. Sixty-one sailors deserted ship. Two others went insane. One committed suicide.

Despite the dangers, *Challenger's* expedition was a great scientific success. For the first time ever the world's oceans were mapped and measured, new species of life were identified, and the ocean waters were investigated as never before.

Extreme Facts

During its amazing three-and-a-half-year voyage, the *Challenger* crew:

- travelled over 110 000 kilometres
- stopped to take depth and temperature readings 362 times
- scooped samples from the ocean floor to depths of over 5000 metres
- discovered 4717 new species of ocean life, including giant worms and slugs, deep-sea shrimp the size of lobsters, and a rare type of squid that wore its skeleton partly inside and partly outside its body
- published a final report that filled 50 volumes (29 500 pages) and took nineteen years of work by seventy-six authors to complete.

City of Gold

It was a legend — a wild, fanciful story — that drew Hiram Bingham to the tangled jungles of Peru and the discovery of a lifetime.

Many years ago, the legend went, a powerful nation of people lived in the high mountains of Peru. The Inca had no written language, yet they were skilled mathematicians and astronomers. They had no iron tools, but they were excellent architects and stonemasons. And although they never discovered the wheel, they built huge stretches of paved road, moved blocks of stone the size of houses, and erected dozens of palaces and temples.

For hundreds of years the Inca ruled Peru, until their conquest by the Spanish in the 1500s. The survivors fled into the mountains where they built a secret city filled with beautiful palaces and stocked with incredible silver and gold treasures. Then, for some reason, they abandoned it, leaving most of the treasure behind. With only the wind to whistle through the city's empty streets, its location was soon forgotten. But stories of its greatness spread across the land, keeping its memory alive . . .

The legend of the Lost City of the Inca intrigued Hiram Bingham, an American university professor. Bingham read books on the Inca, researched ancient documents, examined the records left by Spanish explorers, and studied maps of Peru. Was there really such a marvellous place? he wondered. The only way to track down the truth, he decided, was to visit Peru itself.

In 1911 Bingham led an expedition of six men into the mountains of Peru. For weeks the group trudged up rocky slopes, along narrow trails, and through dense jungles. At every village Bingham asked the same question. Had anyone seen the ruins of an ancient city in the mountains? The answer was always the same — no. Then, on July 23, Bingham heard a different answer. Yes, there were ruins not far away, one man said. He would show Bingham the way.

The next day the native guide led Bingham and one other man farther into the mountains. They followed a narrow, twisting trail that wound through the jungle and skirted a roaring stream. The trail was choked with vines and rocks. Deadly snakes were a constant concern. After hours of difficult travel Bingham suddenly found himself standing at the bottom of a series of terraces lined with fine stones. Like a giant jigsaw puzzle, each stone had been cut and fitted into place.

Bingham's heart began to race. He climbed a stairway that led up the terraces. At the top he found himself at the edge of a huge courtyard. It was the entrance to an ancient city — an incredible city with one huge temple, several smaller temples, and palaces, shops, bathhouses and homes.

The city was perched on top of a mountain like a jewel on a crown. Everywhere Bingham could see the fine craftsmanship of the city's builders. Each stone fitted perfectly into the others. Paved streets curved gracefully around buildings, and private homes lined the way. Marvellous stone steps led to the huge temple that dominated the view.

The natives called the ruins Machu Picchu or "old peak." A fitting name, Bingham thought . . . but was this the Lost City of the Inca? Bingham didn't think so. Neither do modern archaeologists. There was no trace of silver, gold or other treasures. The large number of temples suggested that rather than being a city of kings, Machu Picchu was a religious centre for the Inca, a place to journey to and worship on the high mountain.

Today Machu Picchu stands as a tribute to the genius of the Inca. The Lost City, if there is one, remains hidden in the mountains . . . waiting, perhaps, to be discovered by some future explorer.

Dateline: Science
Solving an Inca Mystery

Much about the Inca is still unknown. Several gruesome discoveries, however, have shed light on their puzzling past. They've also sent scientists scurrying to the mountaintops of Peru in search of more evidence.

In 1954 the body of a seven-year-old boy was discovered frozen in a tomb on a high mountain in Peru. He was dressed in decorative clothes, his hair carefully combed, his face smeared with red and yellow paint. The boy was an Inca and his death was no accident. He had been deliberately placed in the tomb as a sacrifice over 500 years ago.

Then in 1985 another body was found on a different mountain in Peru. This too was the frozen body of a young Inca boy. Like the first, he wore colourful clothes and had been well groomed. His death was no accident, either. He had been suffocated before being entombed on the windswept mountain.

The discoveries caused a stir among archaeologists. Spanish explorers of the sixteenth century told stories of brutal ceremonies in which Inca children were sometimes sacrificed. Many archaeologists had dismissed the stories, thinking these were the imaginative tales of a conquering people. With the discovery of the bodies on the mountains, however, they were left wondering if there was some truth to the stories after all.

In the late twentieth century, archaeologists began venturing into remote mountain reaches of Peru to uncover more evidence. Their work is dangerous and difficult. The climb up steep slopes, burdened with instruments and equipment, is an endurance test of its own. So is excavation work at high altitudes. Winds often whip across the mountain peaks at speeds of 110 kilometres per hour or more. Storms are frequent and temperatures are below freezing. The air is thin and oxygen levels are low. Altitude sickness and constant exhaustion are common problems among high mountain-archaeologists.

But their work has uncovered some startling finds. More than a dozen bodies of Inca children have been discovered on remote mountains in Peru. Some were boys, others girls. Most had died violently before being buried in tombs on the snowy peaks.

Why were the children sacrificed? Why were they buried on remote mountain peaks, in places that were difficult to reach? Most scholars believe that the sacrificed children were offerings to the gods.

Because they were buried on mountaintops where temperatures are continually below freezing, the bodies were actually mummified. That allowed scientists to examine the actual bodies, not just skeletons. The children were unblemished and had obviously been in good health, the most perfect offerings possible. By sacrificing them, the Inca hoped to please the gods. Mountain peaks may have been chosen because they brought the spirits of the sacrificed children closer to heaven.

When were the children sacrificed? Experts have different opinions. Some believe that the sacrifices were made in times of turmoil such as during droughts or eclipses. Others think the children were killed when an emperor or important chief died so that their spirits could be escorted in the afterworld. Still others believe the sacrifices were meant to ensure safe passage through the mountains as the Inca expanded their empire. Like so many other Inca practices, these grim sacrifices remain shrouded in mystery.

Marooned and Desperate

"If anyone has to be eaten, you'll be first," Ernest Shackleton growled to a stowaway who was discovered on board his ship. Fifteen months later, in spite of losing the toes of one foot, the stowaway had Shackleton to thank for not losing a lot more.

Shackleton was the leader of a British expedition that attempted a sea-to-sea crossing of Antarctica. In addition to exploring uncharted territory, the expedition had scientific purposes too. Along the way, scientists hoped to take magnetic readings, study ice formations, collect rocks and soil samples, and examine plant and animals that lived in the harsh climate.

Shackleton and his crew of twenty-nine hand-picked scientists, sailors and craftsmen left England on August 1, 1914, aboard the wooden ship, *Endurance*. They were already far from land when a stowaway was discovered hiding on board. Left with no choice but to continue, Shackleton put him to work alongside the rest of the crew.

After crossing the Antarctic Circle, *Endurance* became locked in ice. For nine months the men waited, unable to move backward or forward. Finally the strain on the wooden ship was too much. The crush of ice burst seams and snapped beams, sinking the ship and leaving its crew stranded on the ice with three lifeboats and a sprinkling of supplies.

Figuring that they were too far away for a rescue, Shackleton came up with a plan: haul their lifeboats across the ice to open sea, then sail north to South Georgia, the nearest inhabited island. The task was easier said than done. In the first five days of heaving and pushing, the men covered only 14 kilometres. They were exhausted and grumbled among themselves about doing away with Shackleton.

Shackleton decided on a second plan. The ice was shifting and drifting northward with the current. Why not stay and ride it out? The men camped on the ice, and for three months fought severe cold, starvation and depression. Finally, in April, they reached open water and put their three lifeboats to sea, heading for the nearest land, a small mass of rock known as Elephant Island.

The crossing took seven days. The lifeboats were cramped, the weather fierce. Unable to camp on the shifting ice, the men slept in the boats, surrounded by killer whales and wayward icebergs that threatened to crush their craft.

But Elephant Island was only a hump of rock in a vast ocean. No one would find them there, Shackleton realized. The two small boats were turned upside down, becoming makeshift shelters. Taking the third boat, Shackleton and a small crew set sail again for South Georgia Island and the whaling stations along its coast.

The journey was a nightmare. Soaked and freezing, starving and thirsty, fighting gales and blizzards, the crew and their battered boat finally reached South Georgia seventeen days later. The men were overjoyed . . . until they realized they had encountered another problem. They had landed on the wrong side of the island! The whaling stations were on the other side. Because their boat was broken and unfit to sail, the only way to get there was to trek 240 kilometres across the snowy mountains in the middle of the island.

Leaving the weakest men behind under the shelter of the overturned boat, Shackleton and two other men started the long journey, stopping for little more than short breaks. On May 20 the men reached a whaling station, shocking the workers, who had assumed that *Endurance* had been lost with all hands.

The men on the other side of South Georgia were rescued shortly after, but because of violent storms it took fourteen more weeks to reach the twenty-two men on Elephant Island. Because of Shackleton's level-headed thinking, they were all there, alive in spite of an ordeal unlike any other. The only real casualty of the two-year adventure was the stowaway. He lost the toes of his left foot to frostbite, but he had Shackleton to thank for saving his life.

Although the Shackleton expedition did not succeed as planned, it did provide other explorers and scientists with valuable information about how to survive in the most severe climate on earth.

Extreme Fact

- In 1997 a team of climbers and sailors built a replica of Shackleton's lifeboat and repeated part of his journey. They climbed several peaks on Elephant Island, sailed the small boat almost 1300 kilometres to South Georgia, and retraced the path taken by Shackleton and his two men as they trekked across the island. The team gained a deeper respect for Shackleton and his crew. As one explorer put it, "Having experienced a small part of what they endured, my respect and admiration for the intrepid trio has gone up tenfold."

Cheating Death

As his rocket-powered aircraft screamed across the California sky on October 14, 1947, Chuck Yeager knew he was cheating death. The plane vibrated violently and threatened to fall apart in mid-air. With each jarring motion, pain shot through his chest from two broken ribs. His right arm ached, too, forcing him to rely on his left to operate the controls. Still he pressed on, firing one engine after the other, climbing higher, determined to reach the speed of sound . . . or die trying.

When scientists have designed a new invention, it sometimes falls to another person to test their theories. This time it was Chuck Yeager's turn. His challenge: break the sound barrier.

An impossible task, some felt. Sound travels at about 1235

kilometres per hour, and pilots who neared this speed reported that their controls locked, the planes shook uncontrollably, and the wings rattled so fiercely that they seemed about to fall off. One British plane had broken apart and crashed. For these reasons many experts believed that there was a wall of turbulence that no aircraft could penetrate, an invisible boundary near the speed of sound, known as the "sound barrier."

To find out if such a barrier existed and if it could be broken, the United States military built a bullet-shaped, rocket-powered experimental plane called the X-1. Then they looked for a pilot to fly it. Chuck Yeager seemed perfect for the job. A twenty-four-year-old U.S. air force captain, Yeager was an experienced pilot known for his quick reflexes, coolness under pressure, love for flying and taste for adventure. Yeager accepted the job in an instant. The opportunity to become the first person to fly faster than the speed of sound was too much to resist.

The plan was to send up the X-1 on a number of flights, each one a little faster than the others, before attempting a final flight at the speed of sound. To save fuel, the X-1 was slung below a B-29 bomber and carried aloft. Only when the B-29 was airborne did Yeager squeeze into its bomb-bay, climb down a small ladder and cram himself feet first through the open hatch of the X-1. At an altitude of 7600 metres the X-1 was dropped. Now clear of the bomber, Yeager fired the engines one by one, boosting the X-1 to tremendous speeds in a few seconds.

The first test flights proved just how dangerous the mission could be. The bomb bay was intensely cold and Yeager's gloved fingers froze and became numb. As the rocket reached high speeds, it rattled and shook, threatening to fall apart. At one point the control wheel jammed, forcing Yeager to grapple with the instrument panel to stabilize the plane.

The Sunday before Yeager was to attempt his final flight in the experiment, he had fallen while horseback-riding and had broken two ribs, as well as injuring his right side. Pushing aside the pain, he went ahead with his flight plans. On the morning of Tuesday,

October 14, 1947, he slowly climbed into the cramped hatch of the X-1. Unable to use his right arm, he used a sawed-off broomstick with his left to close the door to the hatch.

After the X-1 dropped from the bomb bay, Yeager fired the first two engines.

The aircraft bolted across the sky, rocking and bouncing as its speed climbed higher. Then Yeager fired the third engine. The jolting motion stopped. The needles on his instrument panel fluttered, wavered and veered off the scale, indicating that he was flying faster than ever before.

Aircraft workers below heard a giant roar, a sound like booming thunder rolling over the airfield. It was a sound many never expected to hear — the sound of an aircraft flying faster than the sound it produced. The sound of someone breaking the sound barrier.

More Extremes

- Chuck Yeager's record-breaking flight paved the way for other daring tests. Fifteen years later, one of these set a new record and started a revolution in aviation that continues today.

On April 30, 1962, American pilot Joe Walker squeezed into another experimental aircraft known as the X-15. The X-15 was half missile, half airplane. Sleek as a bullet, with tiny wings for lift and control, it was designed to fly to the very limits of the earth's atmosphere. The X-15 was strapped under the wings of a high-flying bomber, then released at a height of 13 700 metres.

Walker flicked a switch to ignite the rocket engines. With a surge of power the X-15 blasted upward. Eighty-two seconds later Walker switched off the engines. Like a rock released from a slingshot, the X-15 soared to an altitude of 75 kilometres. Here, at the very edge of the atmosphere, Walker and the X-15 were just beyond the pull of gravity — and momentarily weightless.

Walker's flight was the first ever of an aircraft into space. His flight, and others using the X-15, pushed the boundaries of flight to the very fringes of space and beyond. Without this

More EXtremes

daring experiment, the space shuttle program that was to follow might never have been possible.

- In 1960 Air Force Captain Joseph Kittinger leaped out of an open balloon gondola almost 30 kilometres above the earth. He plunged through the air at such incredible speeds that he broke the sound barrier, and almost blacked out before his parachute finally opened when he was just over 5000 metres above the ground. Kittinger's jump was part of Project Excelsior, an experimental space program designed to find out how well the human body could withstand extreme-altitude bailouts.

- To be called an astronaut, someone must have flown an aircraft to altitudes above 80 kilometres.

- The greatest altitude ever reached by the X-15 was almost 108 kilometres on August 22, 1963. The pilot? Joe Walker.

To the Bottom of the World

On January 23, 1960, two men — American naval officer Don Walsh and scientist Jacques Piccard — climbed into a floating metal cylinder. Once the door was latched, the two began a dangerous journey into the Pacific Ocean, one that has never been repeated.

The vessel was named *Trieste*. Invented by Auguste Piccard, Jacques' father, *Trieste* was sausage-shaped, with a bubble-like cabin in the middle. It was made of thick steel to withstand tremendous pressure, and had huge propellers on its sides to move it backward or forward under water.

To allow it to rise and sink, *Trieste* was equipped with tanks above and below the cabin. The lower tanks were filled with tiny pellets of iron. Some of the upper tanks held gasoline, which is lighter than water. Others held air. When sea water was allowed into the upper air tanks, the vessel became heavier and started to sink. To reverse the process, iron pellets were released from the lower tank, allowing the gasoline-filled tank to draw the vessel back to the surface.

Early on the morning of January 23, 1960, Walsh and Piccard boarded *Trieste* near the Mariana Islands in the Western Pacific. Their mission was a dangerous one: explore an area of the ocean that was so remote, so isolated and so dark that it had never been visited by humans before. Explore Challenger Deep, part of the Mariana Trench, the deepest trench on earth.

When all was ready, the upper air tanks were opened to allow sea water inside. As its weight increased, *Trieste* began to plunge into the ocean. At 800 metres total blackness engulfed the vessel. The water grew cold, sending a chill throughout the cabin. The two men changed into warm clothing and munched on chocolate bars to keep up their strength.

At 1300 metres *Trieste* sprang a leak, then at 6000 metres, another. Under the enormous pressure building on the surface of the vessel, the leaks actually sealed themselves. An hour passed . . . then two . . . then three. An eerie silence settled over the vessel as it dropped ever deeper into inky blackness.

After hours of steady diving the vessel was shaken by a heavy shock. Next came a sudden thud. Had one of the lights exploded from the tremendous pressure? Had they struck some unknown object? Piccard flipped a switch to light up the floodlamps attached to *Trieste*. Slowly the sea floor came into view. The men realized that they had reached the bottom of Challenger Deep, almost 12 kilometres below the surface. They were at the deepest spot on earth.

To their astonishment, there was life at the bottom of the trench, a place far too deep to be touched by sunlight. Tiny red shrimp, long flatfish and swarms of smaller fish swam by *Trieste*. Piccard also noticed wavy marks in the muddy bottom, perhaps the tracks of some unknown creature.

After twenty minutes the two men released ballast to lighten the vessel, and began the long journey upwards. When they finally came to the surface they climbed out quickly, eager for fresh air. Their epic journey had taken nine hours from start to finish.

More EXtremes

- Don Walsh and Jacques Piccard were not the first explorers to use a specially designed vessel to dive to tremendous depths. Two of the earliest pioneers of deep ocean research were Otis Barton and William Beebe. By cramming themselves into a small hollow steel ball called a bathysphere, and being lowered by cable from a ship, the two made over thirty-five dives into the ocean. Their most famous was on August 15, 1934, when they plunged almost a kilometre below the surface, the greatest depth reached by a human being at that time. Their descriptions of strange fish and wondrous new creatures sparked an interest in ocean research that later scientists continued.

Does daredevil science run in families?
It does for the Piccards.

- In 1932 Auguste Piccard, a Swiss-born
  Belgian physicist, became the first
  person to ride a balloon into the
  stratosphere. To do the job, he
  designed a special sealed cabin below
  the balloon to protect him from the
  cold, thin air.
- In 1960 his son Jacques plunged to the
  deepest point in the Pacific Ocean in
  Trieste, a diving vessel invented by
  Auguste.
- In 1999 Bertrand Piccard, Jacques'
  son, continued the daredevil family
  tradition started by his grandfather.
  He flew *Breitling Orbiter 3,* the first
  balloon to travel non-stop around
  the world.

Dateline: Science
Unravelling the Ocean's Mysteries

More has been discovered about the ocean in the past fifty years
than in the previous five hundred. And for ocean researchers, it's
just the start. High-tech equipment has made the difference. Gone
is the clunky ball used by Barton and Beebee. Even *Trieste* seems
like a slow-moving dinosaur. Today's ocean explorers use
computers, videocameras and robots to help them go deeper, stay
longer and find out more than ever before.

One of the newest devices for deep ocean research is the submersible, a type of mini-submarine. Tough and durable, submersibles are also small and portable. They can dive to great depths, and many are equipped with robotic arms to help the operator retrieve objects from the ocean floor.

Then there's the ROV or Remote Operated Vehicle. Operated much like a remote-control toy car, the ROV is an undersea robot that can go places the submersible cannot. Videocameras attached to the ROV transmit images directly to the operator, enabling the explorer to "see" the action first-hand. Thrusters on the robot allow it to be steered wherever the operator desires.

For long-term study, ocean explorers can spend time in something like Aquarius, a 14-metre-long underwater laboratory that looks like a giant pod moored on the ocean floor. Researchers live in Aquarius for weeks at a stretch. Inside their underwater cocoon they study marine life, monitor temperatures and currents, and conduct experiments.

With the techno-wizardry of submersibles, ROV's and undersea pods, ocean explorers have gone to places that were once considered unreachable. And what they've discovered has dazzled and amazed us.

One of the most shocking discoveries was made in 1977 by scientists aboard the submersible *Alvin*. They were exploring a section of the Mid-Atlantic Ridge, a chain of mountains that winds its way along the bottom of the Atlantic Ocean. This particular section, just off the coast of Ecuador in South America, was volcanically active. Lava oozed from creases and folds in the rock.

Because they were over 3 kilometres below the surface, too far for sunlight to penetrate the water, scientists expected to find few signs of life. They were in for a surprise.

Near lava vents they discovered warm-water springs, and around these, hundreds of bizarre creatures: giant clams, white crabs, bright red shrimp and orange dandelion-shaped fish. Strangest of all were snakelike creatures that stood upright in long tubes. These tube worms had no eyes, no mouths, no means of movement and no apparent way to feed themselves. Somehow, however, they thrived on the ocean floor.

How could these organisms survive without sunlight and without plants? Closer studies showed that near lava vents, the water was acidic and crawling with bacteria that fed off sulphur spewing from the warm-water springs. The bacteria, in turn, became food for all sorts of creatures higher up the food chain.

The discovery showed that not all life forms follow the same rules for survival, and that likely there are other surprises in store for us in the far reaches of the ocean.

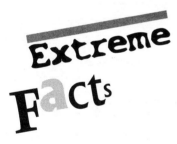

Extreme Facts

- **One of the biggest problems with swimming under water is pressure. (Water is a lot heavier than air, so under the water the pressure is much higher than on land. The deeper you go, the greater the pressure becomes.) It's a problem that plagues divers as well as submarines and other submersibles.**
- **Water pressure pushes on you, squeezing your lungs so that they hold less air than usual. At a depth of 10 metres the pressure is double that on the surface, and your lungs compress to half their usual space. At 30 metres the pressure is four times as great, and your lungs hold one-fourth their normal volume of air. Reduced lung capacity is one reason why divers, even those wearing scuba gear, cannot go to great depths for any length of time.**

Extreme Facts

- At Challenger Deep, part of the world's deepest trench, pressure is immense. When *Trieste* explored the area, the pressure on its surface was estimated to be 180 000 tonnes.
- Sea mammals have far fewer problems with water pressure than humans. When two dogfish sharks (of a species found only on the sea floor) were discovered inside the stomach of a sperm whale, scientists were led to theorize that the sperm whale sometimes descends as deep as 3 kilometres when seeking food.

"I Was Born to Do This."

On her first trip into the jungle, Biruté Galdikas faced crocodiles, snakes and pouring rain. After paddling down a muddy river in a dugout canoe for six hours, she finally reached the ramshackle hut that was to be her home. It was filthy and crawling with insects and vermin.

Many people might have turned around and given up. Not Galdikas. "I was born to do this," she said. "I felt I was coming home."

"Home" for Galdikas had been a typical house in Canada. But for more than twenty-five years she has traded the comforts of modern living for the wilds of the jungle, and the company of humans for that of orangutans.

Galdikas is an anthropologist, a scientist who studies human societies and development. In 1971 she made her first trip to the rainforests of Borneo, convinced that she could learn a great deal about early humans by observing modern day apes. Other scientists had studied chimpanzees and gorillas, but no one had observed orangutans first-hand.

Orangutans live only on the islands of Borneo and Sumatra in Indonesia. Unlike chimpanzees and gorillas, who live in groups and have organized social systems, orangutans like to be left alone. They spend their days in the rainforest canopy, high above ground, moving steadily from tree to tree in search of food. Weeks can pass before one orangutan meets another. Even then the encounters may not be friendly. Often there are snarling and grunting matches, as one orangutan claims territory over the other.

Knowing that the orangutans would not come to her, Galdikas searched for them. She quickly established a routine. Rising at three-thirty each morning, she left her hut and headed into the jungle, often spending the next sixteen hours plodding through dense undergrowth, standing waist-deep in swamps, fighting mosquitoes and leeches the entire way. It was gruelling, exhausting work. At the end of a typical day her shoes and clothing were soaked, her skin was pocked with bites, and bloated leeches had to be wrenched from her body.

Weeks turned into months before Galdikas's perseverence paid off. One day she spotted a mother orangutan and her baby, and managed to follow them through the jungle. She watched the mother build a nest in the trees and bed down with her baby. The next morning, to her surprise, the animals were still there. Galdikas realized that if she could track the animals during the evening, she would find them in the same tree the next morning.

From then on, Galdikas made headway in her research. She recorded her observations in books, charting in detail the movement and behaviour of these animals. Singlehandedly, she discovered more about orangutans than any scientist before her. She found that orangutans eat over 400 different kinds of foods, that mothers care for their babies for eight years, and that although these apes prefer to be alone, they do engage in some social behaviours.

Her discoveries have not come without a price. Over the years, Galdikas developed ulcers on her legs from her long hours in swampy water. More than once she has caught malaria and other deadly diseases. One time after she sat on a log to rest, she suffered severe skin burns from toxic sap that seeped from the wood.

To Galdikas, the rewards far surpass the hardships. Because of her determination, Biruté Galdikas has become the world's leading expert on orangutans, and a leader in the fight to protect this endangered species.

More EXtremes

- In 1960 Jane Goodall arrived in Tanzania to study wild chimpanzees, something many at the time believed to be an unfitting occupation for a woman. Without formal training, but plenty of determination and patience, Goodall gradually became accepted by the chimpanzee community. She began to observe the animals in the wild and to keep detailed records of their behaviours. Her work holds the record as the world's longest continuous field study of animals in their natural habitat.
- Dian Fossey began her work with the mountain gorillas of Rwanda in 1967. At the time there were only a few hundred of these animals left, and poachers posed the greatest threat to their existence. Fossey lived among the gorillas, spending thousands of hours studying their habits and

More Extremes

behaviours in the hopes of understanding them and saving them from extinction. At first the gorillas avoided her, but in 1970 Fossey succeeded where others had failed. Peanuts, an adult male, touched her hand — making this the first friendly gorilla-human contact ever recorded.

Fossey fiercely campaigned for the survival of the mountain gorillas and for an end to poaching, often antagonizing the people who made poaching a profitable business. But she refused to back down, even though she knew her opinions were resented by others. On December 26, 1985, Dian Fossey was murdered. The identity of her killers remains a mystery.

Dateline: Science
Halting Deadly Ebola

Her forehead was hot and sweaty. Her muscles ached too. A touch of the flu, she tried to tell herself, but inside, deep in her gut, this Swiss scientist knew better. And when her nose started to bleed, when cramps gripped her stomach and wouldn't let go, when her thoughts grew hazy and her emotions wild, she knew for sure. She had become infected with the deadly Ebola virus, the very disease she'd been hoping to conquer.

How had she contracted the disease? she wondered. But even before she could voice the question, she knew the answer. For months she'd been investigating mysterious deaths among local chimpanzees along the Ivory Coast in West Africa. Autopsies showed that their organs were masses of bloody, contaminated tissue, a clear sign that the chimps had died of the Ebola virus. Somehow, even though she had taken all the necessary precautions, she had caught the often-fatal disease herself. Fortunately for this researcher, the disease was detected in time. She was evacuated to a hospital in Switzerland, where she recovered.

Most victims of the disease are not so lucky. Ebola takes its toll quickly, causing massive amounts of bleeding, and, in the worst cases, death within six to ten days. Since the first outbreak of Ebola in 1976, nearly a thousand people have died, and despite the best efforts of scientists around the world, no one has been able to find a cure or even a proper explanation for the mysterious disease.

Ebola first surfaced in the countries of Zaire and Sudan in Africa. The disease spread quickly, killing 890 people in a matter of weeks. In 1979 it reappeared in Sudan, then again in Zaire in early 1995. The disease is highly contagious, and exactly where it originated and how it spreads is uncertain. Ebola seems to hide between outbreaks, then crop up again — often in a different location and in a slightly different form. In 1989 a third strain appeared in a West Virginia research facility, in a shipment of monkeys imported from the Philippines. No humans died, but hundreds of monkeys either died or had to be killed to prevent further spread of the virus.

The case of the Swiss researcher who contracted Ebola in November of 1995 may provide some clues. Since then, researchers have been combing the Tai Forest, the region where she first became infected by a diseased chimpanzee. They have captured thousands of birds, mammals and insects. Samples taken from the captured animals are being tested to see if there is a virus linked to Ebola.

Right now, however, there are more questions than answers. Scientists risk their own health by working in the field, and in laboratories around the world, as they continue to search for a cure.

More
EXtremes

- One of the world's worst killers lives under protective custody in Atlanta, Georgia. This killer stalks the young and old, targets the weak and unprotected, deals death swiftly and mercilessly, and has taken millions of lives.

The killer is smallpox, one of the world's most deadly and infectious viruses. For centuries smallpox killed and maimed countless people around the world. Then, in 1796, Edward Jenner discovered the smallpox vaccine, which offered immunity from the disease. Gradually medicine began to conquer the killer. In 1978 smallpox was declared eradicated, wiped off the face of the earth. Almost . . .

Live samples of the microbe are kept at the Center for Disease Control and Prevention (CDC), a research facility in Atlanta, Georgia. Researchers there believe having the live virus on hand is essential. Viruses have a way of becoming resistant to treatments over time. Should the smallpox vaccine ever prove ineffective, the live virus might be just the key to discovering new or more effective medicines.

More EXtremes

Smallpox is not the only deadly virus housed at CDC. Scientists there study Ebola, AIDS, cholera, malaria and dozens of other infectious killers in the hopes of understanding them and finding cures. They conduct their work under the tightest security and with the utmost caution. Still, they are aware of the risks associated with these viruses, and only have to recall an incident that occurred in Africa in 1996 to be reminded of the dangers.

That year, a medical worker treating patients with Ebola unknowingly became infected. While he was being treated for the disease, the virus was transmitted to a nurse. She became violently ill and died.

Even among trained professionals, killer diseases like this can strike when least expected.

Medicine on the Front Lines of Danger

In times of war, disaster, or widespread epidemic, most people flee to safety. Not Doctors Without Borders. They head directly into the troubled area. Doctors Without Borders is a group of volunteer doctors, nurses and specialists who provide medical support to people in places of turmoil. Since its start in France in 1968 as *Médecins sans Frontières*, thousands of volunteers with this agency have defied governments and risked their own personal safety to bring relief to the sick, injured and displaced in eighty countries worldwide.

Volunteers for Doctors Without Borders face danger on a daily basis. Often they work in areas devastated by natural disasters such as earthquakes and floods, where hazards and disease abound. Just as often, they bring aid to people trapped in the world's "hot zones," regions where war and political upheaval have taken their toll in human suffering. In August of 1999, two medical volunteers working with refugees fleeing war-torn Sierra Leone were captured and held prisoner in Liberia. Even though they were safely released a few days later, their plight dramatically illustrated the extreme risks taken by these volunteers who regularly step into the front lines of danger.

In recognition of its valuable contributions, Doctors Without Borders was awarded the Nobel Peace Prize in October, 1999.

4

EXtreme
Solutions

Tackling problems . . .
designing solutions

Imagination is more important than knowledge,
for knowledge is limited.
Imagination encircles the world.

Albert Einstein

Raw patches covered the patient's leg, and every day brought new ones. Worse yet, they'd become infected. Thick pus oozed from the open sores and the sick smell of decay was obvious. Medication hadn't helped. That left two choices, the doctor said. Have the leg amputated to stop the spread of infection . . . or plant maggots in the open wounds as a last desperate solution. Maggots hatch from eggs that are laid by adult flies. These pale, yellow worms grow in warm, inviting places that have plenty of food. They are tiny eating machines, devouring many times their body weight every day.

Certain breeds of maggots crave dead and infected material, and it is their strange appetite that makes them so attractive to some doctors and scientists. These maggots prefer to dine on rotting flesh, leaving healthy tissue untouched. Furthermore, they secrete chemicals that kill harmful bacteria and speed up recovery.

To most people, maggot therapy is repulsive. The thought of deliberately putting tiny, squiggling worms into wounds, then leaving them there to happily munch on their hosts, is revolting. But, drastic as it seems, for some patients the lowly maggot may be the only effective solution.

Solutions to problems are not always easy, simple, popular or obvious. Sometimes the best solution is offbeat, difficult or risky. In short — extreme.

Tackling the British Fleet

Some say Sergeant Ezra Lee was a brave man. Others claim he was foolish. Perhaps he was both.

At the height of the American Revolution, British ships occupied New York harbour. Lee, an American soldier, set out to get rid of at least one of the ships by himself. He aimed to do it with a new and untested vessel, a wooden submarine called the *Turtle*.

The *Turtle* looked like an overgrown radish. Oval-shaped and so small it was a tight fit for even one person, the *Turtle* held a half-hour supply of air — just enough for a very short run underwater. Built by David Bushnell, a bright young inventor, the *Turtle* was also a promising war machine, designed to carry explosives that could be planted in secret among enemy ships. The problem was, Bushnell had never used it, at least not in active combat. Ezra Lee was commissioned to do that.

On September 6, 1776, under the cover of darkness, Lee squeezed himself into the small submarine. Once inside, a lid was locked in place, the *Turtle* was towed upstream, lowered under water, then released. Because there was no motor aboard the vessel, only oars and a rudder for steering, Lee had to rely on the harbour current to make it move. The current dragged the *Turtle* toward the *Eagle*, a sixty-four-gun ship and the pride of the British fleet, until it nudged up against the *Eagle*'s side. Then Lee used one of the *Turtle*'s special features. A hand-operated screw on the inside of the vessel, connected to a long drill outside it, could be used to bore into the wooden hull of the *Eagle*. Lee's hope was to fasten explosives in place.

Lee's first attempt failed, possibly because the drill was trying to pierce a part of the *Eagle*'s hull that was metal-covered. So did his second and third try. Exhausted and running out of air, he cranked the controls and bobbed to the surface . . . right in the midst of the

British ships! The British spotted him and gave chase. Desperate, Lee lit the fuse to a cask of explosives and set it afloat, then headed for shore. Twenty minutes later the powder exploded, shooting a plume of water above the harbour and sending the British fleet into confusion. In that confusion, Lee escaped.

Sergeant Ezra Lee failed in his attempt to sink a British ship, but he did succeed in demonstrating, for the first time, the wartime possibilities of the submarine.

• Although the *Turtle* was not very practical as a war machine, it did have another new feature. Hidden under the operator's seat were sets of tanks. By cranking levers and pushing pedals, the operator opened the tanks to let water in, causing the submarine to sink. By using other controls, the operator pumped water out of the tanks to make the submarine rise. The *Turtle* was the first submarine in history to submerge by filling its tanks with water, a practice followed by even the most modern of today's submarines.

Drake's Folly

The citizens of Titusville, Pennsylvania, laughed themselves silly at Edwin Drake. The man was a nutcase, they figured. For proof, they'd point to a giant hole at the edge of town. It was a hole that Drake had been digging for more than a year, a hole that had already cost him his life savings.

Back in 1857, Edwin Drake had a dream few others in Titusville appreciated. He knew that the ground below the town was rich in oil. The black stuff almost oozed out of the ground on its own. Some of it was getting into wells and finding its way into streams. But Drake wanted to find some way of gathering it into barrels and selling it to fuel companies around the country that were hungry for the stuff.

At first he tried digging out the oil the way miners dug out coal. He shovelled out a deep pit in the ground and tried scooping up the oil. If he was lucky, Drake managed to collect a few litres of oil in a day. More often, the earth around the pit collapsed or the hole filled with water. Hardly the way to become rich, Drake realized, so he tried something else. He hired men to build a shaft into the ground, but when the shaft filled with water Drake abandoned that plan, too.

Then he had a brain wave. People drilled for water, didn't they? Boring a hole into the ground to start a well was common practice. Why not drill for oil instead?

By now Drake was out of money so he started borrowing from friends. The townsfolk shook their heads at the new idea and laughed at him behind his back. They called his plan Drake's Folly.

Undaunted, he hired a local driller to bore a hole into the ground using a steam engine and cast iron pipes. The driller worked day after day, but the pace was slow and there were constant problems. Sometimes the ground caved in. One time the steam engine caught fire.

The people of Titusville laughed even harder and Drake began to see why. After all, he'd spent nineteen months and all of his money digging a useless hole in the ground. Then, just as he was about to give up, his luck changed.

On August 27, 1859, the driller reached a depth of 21 metres and quit for the day. When he returned the next morning, he found oil in the pipe. It was rising from the bottom of the well. Drake was thrilled. His idea worked. The people of Titusville were forced to wipe the smug smiles from their faces, and Drake was ready to receive the rewards of his invention. He offered to sell his secrets to oil companies around the state.

Unfortunately, Drake never reaped the benefits he expected. Because he failed to patent his method of drilling for oil, others copied his technique, never paying him for using it. The inventor died in 1880, almost penniless once again. Dozens of oil companies prospered, however. After they adopted Drake's drilling methods, the oil business boomed. Within a year oil wells across Pennsylvania were pumping half a million barrels of "black gold" out of the ground.

Today Drake is honored for his idea rather than ridiculed. The inscription on a monument in Titusville calls him the Founder of the Petroleum Industry.

The Mask That Saves

One night in 1916, a terrific explosion rocked a tunnel being constructed 86 metres under Lake Erie. Thirty workers were trapped inside. A hastily formed rescue party gathered at the entrance. Fighting thick smoke and clouds of choking gas, they ventured inside. They never returned. Neither did a second rescue party. Or a third.

Then someone remembered Garrett Morgan and his latest invention. Perhaps he could help. A volunteer rushed to Morgan's home and roused him from his sleep. Clad only in pyjama bottoms, he hurried to the scene carrying four strange-looking masks. Quickly he pulled one over his head. Then he convinced his brother and two more volunteers to put on the other masks.

Dressed in the masks, the men looked like aliens from space. Floppy canvas bags completely covered their heads, and dangling rubber hoses ran from the hoods to waterlogged sponges behind. The sponges acted as air filters. They removed impurities and poisons that might otherwise harm the person wearing the hood.

Morgan called the unusual masks "breathing hoods." He had invented them two years earlier after firefighters in his home town of Cleveland, Ohio, had repeatedly been overcome by smoke when putting out fires. Despite their usefulness, however, Morgan had little success convincing people to wear them.

On this particular evening, though, everyone knew that the strange devices were the last hope for the trapped men. Morgan and the three others stepped into an elevator, descended a shaft, and entered the smoke-filled tunnel. The small glass-covered eyepieces made it difficult to see, and the masks were hot and heavy, but they operated as planned — air drawn into them was fresh and clean.

The men groped along the tunnel, occasionally stumbling over rocks and fallen debris.

In a short time they found one of the victims. He was still alive, but choking and struggling for air. Quickly they carried him out of the tunnel, then returned to search for more. Through the night Morgan and his companions pulled several other suffocating workers and rescuers to safety. For most victims, though, it was already too late. The poisonous fumes had taken their toll.

The dramatic rescue made newspaper headlines, and before long Morgan started receiving orders from fire departments for his gas mask. Later, during World War I, it was used to save countless soldiers from poisonous gases on the battlefield.

Saved from a Watery Grave

Charles Momsen arrived on one ship. Allan McCann on another. Both men came for the same reason: to find out if their invention really worked. Seventy-five metres beneath the ocean, thirty-three men depended upon it for their lives.

The *Squalus* was a U.S. submarine. In 1939 it was conducting a training dive off the Atlantic coast when there was a freak accident. An air vent failed, sending water crashing into the engine rooms and crew's quarters, drowning twenty-six men immediately. Quick-thinking survivors sealed off the rest of the ship, but the damage was too great. The weight of water inside *Squalus* plunged the submarine to the ocean bottom, trapping thirty-three bruised and battered men inside.

The survivors sent up emergency flares and a marker buoy. The flares bobbed to the surface, then launched themselves into the air. The marker buoy was attached to a telephone cable and carried a sign saying "Submarine sunk here. Telephone inside."

The submarine was too far down to risk opening the escape hatch and trying to swim to the surface. Without power for lights or warmth, the men sat huddled in the dark, surrounded by silence. Their situation was desperate. They had a limited air supply, and with every exhaled breath the level of poisonous carbon dioxide in the vessel rose. The men had only hours to live.

When *Squalus* failed to contact home base, ships were sent to investigate. Charles Momsen was on board the *Sculpin*. Allan McCann was on the rescue vessel *Falcon*. Although the two men were on separate ships, they shared a common bond. Both had a part in inventing the giant diving bell that rested on *Falcon*'s deck.

The steel bell was called the McCann Rescue Chamber. Large enough to hold nine people, it was designed to be lowered by cable into the water, then sealed in place over the escape hatch of a downed submarine. Once the chamber was in place, the trapped men could leave the submarine, enter the chamber, and be hauled to safety aboard the rescue ship.

At least that was the plan. The problem was that the McCann Chamber had never been fully tested. Not in the rough and tumble waters of the Atlantic. Not to any great depths. Certainly not in an actual rescue situation. Momsen and McCann could only hope that their invention worked as expected. It was the only chance of survival for those who might still be alive aboard the doomed submarine.

The *Sculpin* was the first ship to arrive at the scene. Using the telephone in the marker buoy, the captain contacted the submarine. Then, within minutes, waves rocked the ship, snapping the cable and cutting off all communication. Rescuers aboard the *Sculpin* knew the depth and location of the submarine, but little else.

Inside the submarine, the situation had grown desperate. The temperature had dropped to 4°C. The air, dripping with moisture and stale with carbon dioxide, made the men cold and drowsy. To conserve energy, they huddled under blankets, silent and still, listening to the echoing sounds of *Sculpin* above.

Nineteen hours after the accident, *Falcon* finally arrived. A diver was sent down to secure a cable to the *Squalus*. Two rescuers entered the chamber, then it was winched overboard and lowered into the water. As it disappeared from view, Momsen and McCann watched, anxious questions crowding their minds. Would the chamber buckle under the intense pressure? Would water leak into it, drowning the very men they had come to save? Or, like the telephone line, would the cable snap as the rescue ship rocked on the turbulent ocean, and send its cargo plunging to the bottom?

Metre by metre, the McCann chamber was lowered by cable into the water. When it reached *Squalus* the two rescuers inside guided the chamber into place over the submarine's escape hatch. A special rubber gasket on the underside of the chamber provided a leakproof seal to prevent sea water from entering. Then the hatch was carefully opened. Hoses were inserted, and fresh air was pumped to the men. This was the first stage of the rescue.

Next, seven of the trapped men crawled through the escape hatch into the chamber. The chamber was unlocked, then slowly reeled to the surface. In a short time the survivors were on the deck of *Falcon*, gulping mouthfuls of fresh air while the chamber was lowered for another dive.

On the next two trips, eighteen more men were rescued. Then on the fourth and final trip, the cable began to break and unravel. Fearing that the jerking motion of the winch would snap it, Momsen and McCann decided to raise the chamber up by hand. A team of sailors tugged and heaved, slowly dragging the chamber to the surface. After nearly forty hours trapped underwater, the last eight survivors staggered on board *Falcon*.

The rescue of the *Squalus* crew made diving history. Never before had a rescue attempt been successful from such a great depth.

Extreme Facts

Fate, coincidence or luck?

- While awaiting rescue, all hands aboard *Squalus* were given a specially designed breathing mask to help them overcome the contaminated air. The device was called the Momsen lung — invented by none other than Charles Momsen.

- Six months after it sank, *Squalus* was raised, refitted and renamed *Sailfish*. During World War II it sank a Japanese aircraft carrier. Among the survivors of the sinking were some of the same men that had served on *Sculpin*, the rescue ship. They had been taken prisoner after their own submarine was sunk by the Japanese.

Bombs That Bounce

Torpedoes couldn't do the job. Ordinary bombs dropped from planes couldn't either. But Barnes Wallis's bouncing bomb held promise.

During World War II, German aircraft pounded Britain, dropping a hail of bombs on its cities. To turn the tide of the war, Britain needed to cripple Germany's bomb factories. Most of them were in the Ruhr Valley, a low-lying area fed by rivers and protected by dams. Destroying the dams and flooding the region seemed to be the best way to bring the German war machine to its knees.

But how? The dams were protected by torpedo nets, and bombs dropped from planes tended to roll forward and miss their targets. A more accurate bomb, one that could dodge the torpedo nets and still hit its mark, was needed.

If anyone could produce one, it was Barnes Wallis, a well known aircraft designer and scientist. As he pondered the problem, Wallis remembered a childhood game, skipping stones across the surface of the lake. If stones pitched at just the right angle would bounce and hop across the water, was it possible to do the same with a bomb? Release it at just the right angle, make it skim across the water, bounce over the protective torpedo nets, and land at the base of the dam where it could do the most damage?

Wallis started a series of tests in his laboratory. Using a small catapult he fired marbles across a tub of water. They skimmed the water, but bounced in all directions — spherical shapes, he discovered, moved in unpredictable ways. Next he carved a series of fat, cigar-shaped models and fired these across the water. These flatter, barrel-like shapes worked better. Adding a bit of back-spin as the models left the catapult improved their accuracy even more, and prevented them from plowing into the water.

Many experts ridiculed Wallis. The idea of bouncing explosives seemed too far-fetched. But Wallis ignored his critics. He filled notebooks with detailed measurements and calculations, as he eliminated some designs and perfected others. Finally satisfied that he had enough information, he set about building life-sized bombs to do the job. They were monsters. Weighing as much as two cars, the bombs were almost 2 metres long and more than a metre thick. Each one carried 2722 kilograms of high explosives.

To give the bombs back-spin as they left the plane, a motor rigged to a chain rotated them just before release. Churning at a speed of 500 revolutions per minute, the spinning bombs would hit the water and skip across it rather than plunging down.

Dropping the bombs at just the right angle and height was critical. The problem was solved with two simple flashlights, one fixed in the nose of the plane, the other in the tail.

The flashlights were angled downward so that when the plane was at a height of 18 metres, their beams crossed. When that happened, the pilot knew he was at the proper height to release the bombs.

On May 16, 1943, under the cover of darkness, nineteen planes carrying skip bombs left Britain. Flying low, they swooped over Holland and into German territory. As they approached the dams along the Ruhr Valley, the pilots released their bombs, sending them spinning and skipping across the water.

Barnes Wallis's crazy idea worked. The mission was a success. The skip bombs destroyed two dams, flooding the valley, washing away factories and roads, bringing power and transportation to a standstill. The German war effort ground to a halt.

Extreme Fact

• The first few bombs that were released in the bombing raid of May 16, 1943, failed to strike their targets. One bomb was released late and bounced out of range. Another exploded 70 metres short of its target. The first successful bomb bounced four times before rolling down the face of the dam, exploding and breaking the structure to pieces.

Crisis in the Mediterranean

Panic gripped the world. A bomb was lost. A hydrogen bomb carrying deadly radioactive plutonium!

On January 17, 1966, two U.S., planes, one carrying hydrogen bombs, collided and burst into flames over the Mediterranean Sea. In the debris that rained from the sky, four unarmed hydrogen bombs plunged to earth near Palomares, Spain. The explosive charges in two of these weapons detonated on impact near a farming community, forming craters the size of buildings and scattering radioactive plutonium over the area. A third bomb landed intact in a dry riverbed and was quickly recovered. The fourth bomb fell into the sea and was lost.

Immediately after the disaster, the United States sent 1700 military and scientific workers to begin a massive cleanup of the contaminated area. They excavated and removed tonnes of radioactive soil. They also burned or buried damaged crops.

It was the lost weapon, however, that created an international crisis. No one really knew what damage it had already caused or what threat it really carried. Would its detonator suddenly explode because of the extreme underwater pressure? Would sea water corrode the bomb's protective shell, releasing its radioactive load into the water? Or was the bomb already leaking its deadly poison?

The U.S. Navy sprang into action, determined to find the weapon before damage could be done. Recovery ships steamed to the Mediterranean and divers swept the shallower areas.

Finding the bomb was much like finding a needle in a haystack. It was lost in a region split by deep canyons and sharp drops, some over 1200 metres deep. Ordinary submarines were too bulky and slow to manoeuvre around dangerous obstacles. A smaller, more nimble undersea vessel was needed.

The navy brought in *Alvin*, a speedy, streamlined three-person submersible. Compared to a full-sized submarine, *Alvin* looked puny. But the tiny white sub was packed with the latest in technology. If the bomb could be found at all, *Alvin* would do it. While the world nervously watched and waited, *Alvin* made one difficult dive after another.

But *Alvin* faced immense obstacles. The sea bottom was so covered in thick mud, the crew could sometimes see only 6 metres ahead through the murky water, often even less. Sometimes the submersible's propellers stirred up muck, causing thick clouds to swirl around it. Other times *Alvin* became mired in the mud and had to boot its engines to free itself.

On the nineteenth dive, almost two months after the bomb had been lost, the crew spotted a deep furrow in the mud almost a kilometre below the surface. They tracked it to a steep ravine. The tiny sub followed the furrow, scraping and bumping its way down the slope. Suddenly a ghostly, wavering shape appeared in the searchlights. A parachute. "That's it!" one of the crew shouted.

The bomb lay in a deep gully, the straps and lines still attached, entangled in the parachute that billowed around it like a giant jellyfish. The tangled lines posed a new danger. A slight jar, or too firm a yank, and the bomb might detonate, spewing radiation into the waters around *Alvin* and its crew. Freeing it would be dangerous, too dangerous even for a submersible like *Alvin*.

The navy called for another invention, a robot barely out of the testing stages. The robot, or CURV for Cable Controlled Underwater Recovery Vehicle, looked like an oversized loaf of bread with propellers at one end and a tangle of wires, lights, cameras and a huge mechanical claw at the other. The robot carried no passengers. To operate it, controllers aboard the support ship *Petrel* would send signals through cables attached to the CURV. Cameras on the robot would relay pictures to the crew above.

With *Alvin* hovering nearby, the robot was lowered to the bomb site. It located the parachute and attached two lines to it. Then, before it could attach a third, the bomb started to slip down the ravine. With time running out, the surface controllers drove the robot into the billowing parachutes, entangling it deeply into the fabric. Finally, with the cables from the robot acting as a third line, the bomb was slowly and carefully hauled on board the ship. Everyone knew what could happen if the bomb were jarred.

Other than a few dents and scrapes, the bomb survived the ordeal. The robot had proved its worth. But the real survivors were the crews of the *Alvin* and *Petrel*, who owed the robot their lives. The world, in turn, owed them a debt of gratitude for their courage in pulling off such a dangerous and difficult recovery. People the world over breathed a sigh of relief as the crisis came to a close.

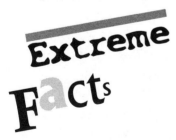

Extreme Facts

Before the high-tech era of robots, people had to make do with different solutions to problems.

• In World War I generals kept in touch with men in the trenches by using carrier pigeons to fly messages back and forth.

• NATO forces stationed in West

Germany in the 1950s sometimes used geese to serve as honking watchdogs.

- The U.S. Navy has trained dolphins and killer whales to locate missiles, find divers, transmit messages and even fend off sharks.
- The K-9 Land Mine Detection Unit, a branch of the U.S. military, uses dogs to find metal and plastic land mines buried underground. The dogs, with a sense of smell a hundred times greater than a human's, can also locate the safest paths through mine fields to rescue soldiers and civilians trapped there.

Dateline: Science
Going Where Humans Can't

In 1994, when scientists wanted to explore an active volcano in Alaska called Mount Spurr, they didn't send one of their own into its steep crater. They sent Dante II, an eight-legged tethered robot, instead.

And when *Mars Pathfinder* landed on the "red planet" in 1997, the hero of the mission wasn't human. It was a six-wheeled, camera-equipped, paperback-sized robot known as LandRover.

LandRover rumbled over the Martian countryside, dodging rocks and outcroppings, transmitting pictures at lightning speed to fascinated earthlings millions of kilometres away.

More and more, robots are being used in place of humans. When new worlds are to be explored, when lives are at stake, when costs are a factor, when pinpoint accuracy is required, robots can be designed to do the job faster and more efficiently. And the next generation of robots will be capable of even more amazing things.

Visit one robotics laboratory and you'll get a glimpse of the future. There you'll find men and women in jeans and T-shirts, hunched over computers, surrounded by wires, filaments, microchips and assorted metal and plastic parts — everything from wheels to infrared transmitters. The centre of attention, however, is not the humans in the room. It's tiny "creatures" that move along the floor — microrobots.

These robots are small — 2 or 3 centimetres in length — but they're packed with miniaturized electrical, mechanical and computerized equipment. Some of the wheeled microrobots dart across the floor, turning tight corners with ease. Other microrobots look like insects. Their six legs let them creep and crawl over and around obstacles in their path.

At first the microrobots move helter-skelter along the floor. But when one of the technicians drops a small object into their midst, a nearby microrobot spots it and emits a signal. That draws the attention of a second microrobot that also emits a signal. Before long, a third, then a fourth and fifth microrobot surround the object. They seem to be talking to one another. When one calls, the others come scurrying to its aid.

Not only are designers trying to make robots smaller, faster and more efficient, they're trying to make them think and act more like people, too. If they are successful, the next generation of robots will function like a team. They'll communicate with one another, share information, solve problems — even make decisions without directions from a human operator.

130

More Extremes

- Possibly the first robot ever created was an artificial duck invented by Jacques de Vaucanson in 1738. His lifelike duck quacked, swam, flapped its wings, smoothed its feathers, drank water with its beak, and even ate grain.
- Sony has taken the concept of a "smart" robot one step closer to reality. They've produced AIBO, a robot dog designed to be a home entertainment pet. AIBO (the word means pal in Japanese) can think, grow, make decisions, communicate with its owner, and express emotions through sounds and actions. All this is possible because of built-in colour cameras, touch sensors, stereo microphones, and a 64-bit computer processor.
- Centaur II, a waterproof robot that moves on caterpillar tracks like a small tank, is used in nuclear plants in emergency situations where radiation levels might be unsafe for humans.

Last Chance for Life

Barney Clark was dying. His heartbeat was rapid and weak. His skin was turning blue, and fluid was collecting in his lungs. Each breath sounded as if it might be his last.

For William DeVries, Clark's doctor, the choices were few. His patient was beyond medication or normal surgery. It was time to try something drastic — remove Clark's heart and give him another one. But the replacement heart DeVries had in mind was not made of human tissue. It was constructed of plastic and aluminum, and it had never been used in a person before.

Barney Clark had once joked that he wouldn't mind being the hundredth recipient of an artificial heart, one that had been tested many times before. He just didn't want to be the first. Now with his heart failing and his condition critical, there appeared to be no other options. Be the first and perhaps survive. Or do nothing and face certain death. "It's time," he finally whispered as he gave permission for the operation to begin.

Late in the evening of December 1, 1982, Barney Clark, a sixty-one-year-old retired dentist, was wheeled into the operating room at the University of Utah hospital in Salt Lake City.

Assisted by a team of fourteen surgeons, nurses and technicians. Dr. DeVries began the delicate operation that might save Clark's life. Standing nearby — ready to give help if it was needed — was Robert Jarvik, the doctor who had invented the artificial heart that would be implanted in Clark's chest. The artificial heart was called the Jarvik-7. It was slightly larger than a human heart, but weighed about the same. It had an aluminum base and two hollow chambers made of plastic. Stretched across the bottoms of the chambers were thin polyurethane diaphragms. Dangling from them, like tassels on a lampshade, were two flexible plastic tubes, 1.8 metres long.

DeVries made a 46-centimetre cut in Clark's chest to expose his heart. Its condition was shocking. His heart was about twice its normal size, and so soft and fragile that it looked like it might stop at any second. Quickly the surgical team hooked Clark up to a heart-lung machine that would keep his blood pumping during the operation. DeVries was now at the point of no return. So was Clark: without a replacement heart, he could not survive. Dr. DeVries cut away the diseased heart and removed it from Barney Clark's chest. Now there was no turning back.

DeVries's next move was to sew special fittings to the blood vessels that remained in Clark's body. The walls of the vessels were so thin and weak that it took almost two hours to do the job. Then DeVries began the delicate task of attaching the Jarvik-7 to the fittings.

To power the heart, DeVries cut small openings in Clark's abdomen just below the rib cage, threaded the long dangling plastic tubes from the Jarvik-7 through the openings, and hooked them up to a large machine known as a heart driver. Once it was turned on, the heart driver — a bulky air compressor on wheels — would pump air through the tubes and force blood into Clark's heart.

When all was ready, DeVries switched on the heart driver. The right side of the heart pumped properly. The left side didn't. DeVries took the Jarvik-7 out, checked all its connections, reinserted it in Clark's chest and tried again. Once more, the pressure was too low. The left side of the Jarvik-7 was clearly defective. Fortunately, the surgical team had planned for an event such as this. DeVries removed the left side of the Jarvik-7, and replaced it with another. The new one worked perfectly.

The operation lasted most of the night. After seven-and-a-half hours in the operating room, Clark was taken to the intensive care unit where his health could be monitored. Gradually his condition improved. His skin colour returned to a normal healthy pink, and the fluid in his lungs slowly drained. By the afternoon, he was awake and alert.

Although the Jarvik-7 worked well, other complications arose in the following months. Clark's condition wavered, then deteriorated. On March 23, 1983, he died of kidney failure with Dr. DeVries and Dr. Jarvik at his side.

Since that time there have been many improvements to the artificial heart to make it more reliable and less bulky. There have been other transplants, too, but the success rate has not been good. Many of the patients have died within days or weeks. One survived almost two years — the longest on record. Their deaths were not a result of mechanical failure or problems with the artificial heart itself, but from side effects such as blood clots, strokes, infection and kidney failure.

Until the success rate improves, the artificial heart remains a temporary measure at best and only a stepping stone to a more lasting solution.

More EXtremes

- The first artificial kidney was a clumsy but effective machine. Invented by a Dutch doctor, Willem Kolff, it was made of over 18 metres of cellophane tubing inside an aluminum drum. Using a process known as dialysis, blood from the patient entered the tubing, then was spun around the drum to draw out impurities before being transfused back into the patient. The first successful demonstration of the artificial kidney was on March 17, 1943. Since then it has been made cheaper, simpler and compact, as well as more portable, allowing those undergoing dialysis to lead lives that are closer to normal.

More Extremes

Finding a way to help those whose organs have failed has intrigued doctors for hundreds of years.

- In 1667, Jean Baptiste Denis injected one litre of lamb blood directly into a young man in an attempt to perform the world's first blood transfusion. He repeated the process on other patients, but eventually faced a charge of manslaughter when one of his patients died. Further attempts were outlawed. Centuries passed before transfusions were attempted again, and it was only after scientists were able to figure out the chemistry of blood groups that the practice was deemed safe.
- In 1912 Alexis Carrel and Charles Guthrie performed the first experimental heart transplant. They transplanted the heart of a small dog into the neck of a larger one.
- Dr. Christiaan Barnard performed the first human heart transplant. On December 3, 1967, he placed the heart of a fatally injured young woman into the chest of fifty-three-year-old Louis Washkansky. The patient lived for only eighteen days, but over the years the success of heart transplants has improved tremendously to give hundreds of desperate people a chance to live.

More EXtremes

- On October 26, 1984, Dr. Leonard L. Bailey of California transplanted a baboon's heart into an infant girl known only as "Baby Fae." The baby had been born with a deformed heart and was sinking fast. Because no human donor was available, Bailey replaced her heart with the only one possible — a baboon's. Unfortunately, Baby Fae lived for only a short time after the operation, but the experience showed that animal-to-human transplants might hold promise in the future.

- Because of a shortage of human organ donations, medical researchers are looking at using pig organs in their place. Pig organs are roughly the same size as human organs, but are more readily available. One major obstacle yet to overcome, however, is organ rejection. Cells in the body tend to try to kill off foreign tissue — that's their usual way of protecting us from infection — but scientists are working on a remedy. They are experimenting with new proteins that would keep the body's cells from recognizing that the pig organ is foreign, so they wouldn't attempt to attack it.

- In 1996, Doctor Ian Wilmut and researchers at the Roslin Institute in

More Extremes

Scotland used cells taken from a six-year-old ewe to clone the world's first mammal, a sheep named Dolly. In cloning, the genes in each cell are duplicated to produce exact copies of the original. Although Dolly was a laboratory copy of her mother, she seemed to be normal in every way. In April of 1998, she gave birth to a healthy female lamb of her own.

However, new research has shown that Dolly and other sheep cloned since then may be aging more quickly than expected, especially animals cloned from cells that have been stored for long periods of time. This has scientists asking the new questions: Are there time limits on how long cells can be stored for cloning?

The ability to manipulate and duplicate cells has raised a storm of controversy. Some people feel that genetic research holds great promise for the future. It may be the key to erasing genetically transmitted diseases, or improving the odds of successful organ transplants. For others, cloning and other types of genetic manipulation are ethical issues. They argue that these practices are dangerous and that they threaten human individuality and freedoms.

Dateline: Science
Designing Superman

Hamayoon Kazerooni is no Arnold Schwarzenegger. He doesn't pump iron, and his biceps aren't the size of tree trunks. But he can lift 227 kilograms with one arm. With a little help, that is.

Hamayoon Kazerooni is an engineer with interests in robotics, medical systems and machines. He is the leader of a team at the University of Berkeley in California that is working on contraptions known as human amplifiers. Worn like clothing, human amplifiers act as extensions of the body and mind, allowing the user to accomplish some amazing feats.

Take the arm amplifier. It looks like it has been torn off some gigantic robot. It's a complicated maze of cables, heavy motors and hydraulics. But when Kazerooni slips his hand into a glove inside the machine, the bulky device roars to life. By squeezing his hand, twisting and bending his arm, swivelling his shoulder and wrist, Kazerooni guides and controls the amplifier. It moves effortlessly, grabs a 227-kilogram steel bar and hoists it high in the air.

Human amplifiers have been in the works for more than forty years. Unlike robots, they aren't controlled by keyboards or joysticks. They're worn, and that allows the amplifier to respond directly to each movement of the controller. In return, the controller feels each movement of the amplifier.

Engineers have high hopes for these devices. Their ultimate dream is to build a full-body amplifier, a sort of superman suit that duplicates the movements of the entire body. One day, not too far in the future, they hope to see it used by disabled people, allowing them to accomplish tasks that might normally be impossible, or by workers in factories, shipyards, airports, construction sites and nuclear power plants — any place where heavy loads need to be moved quickly and precisely.

Extreme Facts

Over the years, engineers, doctors and inventors have concocted some amazing ways of improving lives, and sometimes even saving them.

- In 1505 a German knight had his right arm shot off in battle. A local metalworker came to his rescue. He fashioned a moveable artificial arm for the knight, complete with jointed fingers which could be opened, closed and wrapped around objects to lift them. With his artificial arm, the knight returned to his former duties with a new title, the Knight of the Iron Hand.

- In 1927 Philip Drinker, a university professor, fashioned an unusual machine from two vacuum cleaners and other odds and ends. The machine was called an iron lung, and it proved its worth almost immediately. On October 12, 1928, it was tested on a young girl in Boston, Massachusetts. The girl was a polio victim who could not breathe on her own. The vacuum cleaners in Drinker's device used air pressure to force air into and out of her chest, showing that the iron lung could be used to keep polio victims alive.

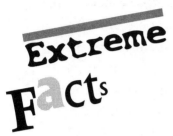

- Sometimes old remedies are found to have current uses. From the time of ancient Egypt, right up to the mid-1800s, it was thought that "bleeding" a person could be an effective treatment for anything from headaches to gout. Leeches would be applied to the affected area to suck out the blood. Strangely enough, leeches are still used today. One company supplies over 20 000 leeches per year, around the world, to medical people who need the leeches' help to restore blood circulation to grafted tissue. The leech can remove the congested blood, so that fresh blood flows freely again. In 1985 surgeons used leeches to save a young boy's ear after it had been bitten off by a dog.
- Many burn victims die because they lack a protective skin covering to keep body fluids in and lock bacteria out. Burn victims were helped immensely in 1981 when John Burre, a surgeon, and Ioannis Yannas, an engineer, announced that they had developed artificial skin. Artificial skin has an inner layer of cowhide and shark cartilage and an outer layer of sticky plastic, and acts like a living patch. When laid on burned areas, it allows nerves and blood vessels to grow into it.

Building Busters

Do you have a thirty-one-storey building you want demolished? You could dismantle it piece by piece, a job that would take many months, require a hundred workers, and send your costs skyrocketing. Or you could call Mark Loizeaux. He and his crew will have it down with the press of a button.

Mark Loizeaux is president of Controlled Demolition, Inc. (CDI), a company that specializes in imploding structures. Mark's father, Jack, pioneered the process of using explosives to collapse buildings, making them fold in on themselves, wall by wall, brick by brick.

Imploding a building is not as easy as it sounds. It requires careful planning and a complete understanding of explosives and structural materials. To do the job right, the CDI crew need backgrounds in engineering, architecture, geology, chemistry and physics. Explosives have to be strategically placed, then set and detonated at precise intervals so that the building collapses on itself much like a house of cards. Too powerful or quick an explosion and the blast might damage surrounding buildings or injure people in the neighbourhood. Too weak or slow an explosion, and the building will only partially collapse, forcing crews to enter a weakened and dangerous structure to finish the job.

On October 24, 1998, in front of a crowd of 20 000 spectators, CDI dropped the thirty-one-storey J.L. Hudson Department Store in

Detroit, Michigan, to the ground, collapsing it into a neat pile of rubble 11 metres tall and several city blocks wide.

It took only seconds to bring the building down . . . but it took seven months to prepare for the event. First, a twenty-one-person crew investigated the complex. They examined blueprints, checked the structural underpinnings of the building, and determined exactly what kind of explosives to use and where to place them. The store's foundation was reinforced to support the walls that would collapse upon it, and steel beams inside the building were partially severed using cutting torches. Later, a crew spent twenty-four days planting the explosives. In all, 4118 separate charges — a total of 1237 kilograms of explosives — were placed in 1100 different locations.

At 5:47 p.m. on October 24 the mayor of Detroit pressed a button to start the implosion. Explosives in one end of the structure fired first, causing one corner section to sag. Within seconds, explosive charges in other sections were fired. Like a wave of destruction, the building crumpled upon itself, one section dragging the next to the ground until the whole structure was reduced to a heap of broken steel and concrete.

In the past five decades, CDI has levelled over 7000 structures around the world, making the Loizeaux family leaders in controlled destruction.

Although implosion experts use many hi-tech devices, some of their tools are decidedly low-tech too. In order to make sure no one is in a building after explosives have been planted and beams have been cut, a member of the crew sometimes starts at the top floor and works down the stairs, sprinkling ordinary household flour on the steps. That way, the footprints of anyone entering the dangerous building will be seen, and the person evacuated before the building is dropped.

Extreme Facts

CDI has established a batch of world records for its explosive work:

- October 24, 1998: Dropped the J.L. Hudson Department Store. Records: the tallest building and largest in area ever imploded
- August 16, 1998: Imploded seventeen apartment buildings in San Juan, Puerto Rico, the tallest being thirteen stories. Record: most buildings brought down in a single implosion sequence
- June 23, 1998: Downed the Omega Radio Tower in Trelew, Argentina. Record: At 366 metres, the tallest man-made structure ever destroyed with explosives
- March 16, 1980: Dropped the Parkersburg-Belpre Bridge in West Virginia. Record: At 861 metres, the longest suspension bridge ever felled.

Operation Desert Hell

Kuwait was on fire!

In the final days of Operation Desert Storm, when Iraqi president Saddam Hussein sensed defeat, his troops set fire to over 500 Kuwaiti oil wells as a final insult to the country they had invaded. From every direction black smoke swirled into the sky, blotting out the sun and spewing contamination into the atmosphere. In short order, desert winds whipped the pollution around the globe. Oily dust settled on streets entire continents away.

To combat the inferno, firefighting teams from the United States, Canada and Kuwait sprang into action. The firefighters had years of experience, but no one had ever encountered a situation like this. Killing a single oil well fire was difficult enough. Killing hundreds of them in a remote war-torn country seemed impossible. Many predicted it would take years to do the job — too long to save Kuwait and its surrounding areas from ecological disaster. The monumental mission was dubbed Operation Desert Hell.

The act of snuffing out any raging fire is, in fact, part art and part science. Firefighters need patience, determination and sheer guts, but also an understanding of fires and how they work. All fires need two ingredients to keep them going: fuel and oxygen. Fires are extinguished by removing one or both: cut off the fuel supply . . . smother the flames.

Oil well fires, though, are trickier than most. For one thing, they have an almost endless supply of underground fuel. The fuel is highly unstable, too — a single spark can set off a massive explosion. And getting close enough to the raging fire to smother it is no simple matter. The burning oil creates a mound of rock-hard debris around the wellhead. To get at the flames, the mound has to be broken and the wellhead exposed, a difficult task when the heat from the fire is so intense it chars the soles of shoes and scorches the clothes of anyone who approaches.

The fires in Kuwait posed other risks too. Sticky pools of oil, some the size of small lakes, covered the ground. Mines and unexploded bombs littered the countryside. Many were covered with oil, making them difficult to detect. One false move could set off a chain reaction, leaving even more death and destruction in its wake.

The firefighters tackled the problems, one oil well at a time. To get close to the flames they used specially equipped tractors with 20-metre-long booms. After rolling into position, they scraped the mound with the boom, gradually wearing it down until it collapsed. Then with the wellhead exposed, they set about squelching the fire. Usually, huge volumes of sea water were dumped on the fire to smother it. Other times foam was lathered on the flames to put them out. In extreme cases dynamite was used to blast the fire into submission — a dangerous practice where explosive materials like oil abound. The dynamite snuffs out the fire by depriving it of the oxygen it needs to burn.

The final step — sealing the wellhead — proved to be the most dangerous of all. Even though the fire was out, oil still shot skyward, spreading a shower of fumes and fuel into the air. A stray spark, a single glowing ember, could ignite the well again, causing an explosion and endangering those nearby. Working as quickly as possible, firefighters would lower a special pipe over the wellhead, bolt it in place, then crank its valves to seal the well and finish the job.

Despite the dangers and difficulties, the monumental task of killing and capping more than 500 fires was completed in record time. By October of 1991, eight months after its start, Operation Desert Hell was over.

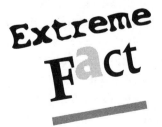

• At the height of the disaster, the fires of Kuwait were consuming more than six million barrels of oil a day. The total cost to Kuwait was estimated to be over $5 billion.

Looking Forward

Remember Giordano Bruno, the Italian astronomer burned at the stake in 1600 for daring to state that there might be life on other planets? Bruno would be happy to know that the question he died for is still in the minds of curious scientists, four centuries later.

Eavesdropping on the Neighbours

Astronomer Frank Drake hoped his neighbours would be noisy. Not the neighbours next door or the ones down the block. The neighbours across the galaxy, a hundred light years away. With any luck, he'd be able to eavesdrop on their conversations.

Drake wondered if there was intelligent life elsewhere in the universe, and if so, how would we know? He figured the evidence was not to be found on earth in the form of flying saucers and little green men. The evidence would be in space in a form that was a lot less visible and, to some, even stranger.

Drake knew that distant objects in space — stars, planets, galaxies — give off a steady stream of invisible energies, everything from X-rays to gamma rays. In fact, detecting these signals was part of Drake's job. He operated a radio telescope in California, and each day he charted and recorded microwave radio signals that filtered in from space.

If there were intelligent life forms in far-flung galaxies, wouldn't they communicate with each other? Wouldn't they try sending messages to other civilizations? Drake believed they would. The easiest way to detect extraterrestrial life, he figured, was to locate their radio signals. In 1960 he started a search for extraterrestrial intelligence, called Project Ozma after a character in the *Wizard of Oz* books. Since space is a huge frontier, Drake narrowed down his search. He turned his radio telescope toward two nearby stars, Epsilon Eridani and Tau Ceti. Then, because radio signals come in many frequencies, Drake tuned his radio to one he thought other civilizations might use, 1420 megahertz — the frequency of hydrogen, the most common element in the universe.

The first star he studied showed no signals at all. The second was more promising. Drake detected a strange, steady signal coming from it. When he turned the telescope away from the star, the signal disappeared. Was the broadcast signal from another civilization?

For days Drake tracked the radio signal, his hopes rising. Then they were unexpectedly dashed when he found that the signal didn't come from the star after all. His telescope had picked up stray signals from a military experiment instead.

Although Frank Drake didn't detect signals from other civilizations, his idea of using radio telescopes to search for extraterrestrial intelligence (SETI) gradually became accepted by others. Today many people who scoffed at the possibility of extraterrestrial life forms are less certain of themselves.

One reason may be that new planets *have* been detected around stars in distant galaxies. Some of them seem to have conditions that are necessary to support life. Chances are greater than ever that at least one remote planet may have intelligent life on it.

Another reason may be the mysterious signals detected by SETI scientists. In 1977 a strong signal was recorded by scientists at Ohio State University. The signal was clear and much louder than other noises detected from space. The operator wrote "WOW" on the record chart. The "Wow" signal, as it came to be called, was exactly the kind of signal astronomers expected would be sent by another civilization.

Unfortunately, bleeps like this are rare. So far there have never been more than one of them at any particular time. With so little data, scientists have been forced to assume that the strange sounds come from a source on our own planet rather than from outer space.

Dateline: Science
Join the Search for E.T.

Since the time of Project Ozma, dozens of other scientists have taken up the challenge of SETI and have aimed their telescopes at the sky. These scientists believe they are very close to a major breakthrough, so their work continues with more enthusiasm than ever. One of their most ambitious undertakings is Project Phoenix. Over the next decade, scientists plan a thorough survey of space, involving a targeted search of 1000 nearby sun-like stars. These stars are within 200 light years of earth and are the mostly likely to have planets capable of supporting life. Using some of the world's largest radio telescopes, scientists will "listen" to millions of radio channels in the hopes of finding telltale bleeps from distant civilizations. If they do, the fun will just be starting. Once we have a clear message from our neighbours, we will start looking for ways to reply.

Analyzing the data from telescopes around the world requires a great amount of computer power, far more than SETI scientists have available. With SETI@Home, scientists hope to "borrow" your computer to help them out at times when you're not using it. By using a screen saver that is capable of retrieving, analyzing and reporting SETI data, you and your computer can help scientists unravel the mysteries of space.

INDEX

Selected Bibliography

Baker, Daniel B., ed. *Explorers and Discoverers of the World*. Detroit: Gale Research Inc., 1993.

Billings, Henry and Melissa. *Daredevils*. Lincolnwood, Illinois: Jamestown Publishers, 1996.

Billings, Henry and Melissa. *Weird Science*. Lincolnwood, Illinois: Jamestown Publishers, 1996.

Crooke, Bette and Charles L. *Famous Firsts in Medicine*. New York: G.P. Putnam's Sons, 1974.

Davidson, Jesse. *Famous Firsts in Aviation*. New York: G.P. Putnam's Sons, 1974.

Dowswell, Paul. *Tales of Real Adventure*. London: Usborne Publishing, Ltd., 1996.

Giscard d'Estaing, Valerie-Anne. *Inventions and Discoveries*. New York: Facts On File, 1993.

Hathaway, Nancy. *The Friendly Guide to the Universe*. New York: Penguin Books Ltd., 1994.

Jeffries, David. *The First Flyers*. New York: Franklin Watts, 1987.

Kane, Joseph Nathan. *Famous First Facts*. New York: H.W. Wilson Co., 1981.

Lomask, Milton. *Great Lives: Explorations*. New York: Charles Scribner's Sons, 1988.

McGovern, Ann. *Shark Lady: True Adventures of Eugenie Clark*. New York: Scholastic Book Services, 1978.

Robertson, Patrick. *The Book of Firsts*. New York: Clarkson N. Potter, Inc., 1974.

Reader's Digest Association. *Great Adventures That Changed Our World*. New York: The Reader's Digest Association, Inc., 1978.

WEB SITES OF INTEREST

GENERAL SITES
Check these all-round useful sites for the latest developments in science and technology as well as further links to other sites.

Discovery Channel Online
http://www.discovery.com/

NASA Home Page
http://www.nasa.gov/

National Geographic
http://www.nationalgeographic.com/

Nova Online
http://www.pbs.org/wgbh/nova/adventures/

Popular Mechanics
http://www.popularmechanics.com/

Popular Science
http://www.popsci.com/

SPECIAL SITES FOR SPECIAL INTERESTS
Controlled Demolition Inc. Home Page
Click on World Records for info on their most challenging projects.
http://www.controlled-demolition.com/

Discovery Channel Online: The Ice Never Sleeps
Icebergs and the measures science has taken to ensure safety at sea.
http://www.discovery.com/exp/icebergs/ice101.html

National Center for Disease Control and Prevention
The work being done with infectious disease at the Atlanta research centre.
http://www.cdc.gov/ncidod/index.htm

The JASON Project
Includes links to ongoing undersea research, online activities, video and more.
http://www.jasonproject.org/

SETI Online
The home page of the SETI Institute with links to specialists and projects.
http://www.seti-inst.edu/Welcome.html

The South Pole Adventure Web Page
The latest on experiments and activities being conducted at the South Pole.
http://astro.uchicago.edu/cara/southpole.edu/

The Tornado Project Online
Your link to storm-chasing activities. Includes information about disasters, personal safety, myths and the science behind tornadoes.
http://www.tornadoproject.com/